Establishing an Experimental Community College in the United States

This text offers an in-depth case study of the development of an experimental community college established by City University of New York with the aim of increasing two-year completion rates. By detailing academic and administrative reforms undertaken at Guttman Community College since 2007, the text illustrates the implementation of innovative practices in developmental education, advising, and experiential education and offers critical commentary on why reforms failed to bring the expected results.

In a series of comprehensive and insightful chapters, Jordan maps the process of implementation and reform at Guttman Community College. In doing so, he explores the shortcomings of the Guttman enterprise and offers an in-depth analysis of the causes and implications of a failure to account for the local context and student population in the planning and implementation phases. This unique, historical narrative thus offers important insights into pitfalls and best practices around issues of racial inequity, governance and leadership, curriculum development, student support services, and data-driven decision-making. Each chapter concludes with a section focusing specifically on implications for the postsecondary system more broadly to inform effective, appropriate, and inclusive college reform.

This book will be of interest to postgraduates and researchers exploring the history and governance of postsecondary education in the United States, as well as academic administrators, faculty, and policymakers. Jordan speaks to the myriad lessons that can be valuable for a higher education landscape that is hungry for innovation and reform.

Chet Jordan is Dean of Social Sciences and Professional Studies at Greenfield Community College, USA.

Routledge Research in Higher Education

Management Behaviours in Higher Education
Lessons from Education, Business and Sport
David Dunbar

The Impact of Higher Education Ranking Systems on Universities
Kevin John Downing, Petrus Johannes Loock and Sarah Gravett

Humanizing Grief in Higher Education
Narratives for Allyship and Hope
Edited by Nicole Sieben and Stephanie Anne Shelton

Human Resource Perspectives on Workplace Bullying in Higher Education
Understanding Vulnerable Employees' Experiences
Leah P. Hollis

Higher Education in the Gulf
Quality Drivers
Edited by Reynaldo Gacho Segumpan and John McAlaney

Establishing an Experimental Community College in the United States
Challenges, Successes, and Implications for Higher Education
Chet Jordan

Research Methods in English Medium Instruction
Edited by Jack K.H. Pun and Samantha M. Curle

For more information about this series, please visit: www.routledge.com/Routledge-Research-in-Higher-Education/book-series/RRHE

Establishing an Experimental Community College in the United States

Challenges, Successes, and Implications for Higher Education

Chet Jordan

NEW YORK AND LONDON

First published 2022
by Routledge
605 Third Avenue, New York, NY 10158

and by Routledge
2 Park Square, Milton Park, Abingdon, Oxon, OX14 4RN

Routledge is an imprint of the Taylor & Francis Group, an informa business

© 2022 Taylor & Francis

The right of Chet Jordan to be identified as author of this work has been asserted by him in accordance with sections 77 and 78 of the Copyright, Designs and Patents Act 1988.

All rights reserved. No part of this book may be reprinted or reproduced or utilised in any form or by any electronic, mechanical, or other means, now known or hereafter invented, including photocopying and recording, or in any information storage or retrieval system, without permission in writing from the publishers.

Trademark notice: Product or corporate names may be trademarks or registered trademarks, and are used only for identification and explanation without intent to infringe.

Library of Congress Cataloging-in-Publication Data
A catalog record for this book has been requested

ISBN: 978-0-367-50944-6 (hbk)
ISBN: 978-1-032-05971-6 (pbk)
ISBN: 978-1-003-05193-0 (ebk)

Typeset in Bembo
by Apex CoVantage, LLC

This book is dedicated to my forever friend,
Dr. Lavita McMath Turner.

Contents

Acknowledgments viii
Preface x
Foreword xiii

   Introduction 1

1 The Planning Stage 14

2 From Concept to College 29

3 Issues of Administration and Governance 53

4 Curricular Challenges 69

5 Revising the Model 84

6 The Way Forward 98

   Afterword 110

   Index 113

Acknowledgments

This book is very appropriately dedicated to Dr. Lavita McMath Turner. When Lavita joined us at Guttman, the college entered a long period of reform in large part due to her unwavering commitment to human rights and educational equity. In so many wonderful ways, Lavita has taught me how to be brave and the virtue of rigorous honesty. We have been on a complicated journey together, one that has been both fulfilling and terribly difficult. Lavita has deeply influenced the content of the book and the ways in which I explain the challenges Guttman has faced. I am endlessly grateful for her love, support, and friendship over these years, and I can't imagine a more special person to whom this book should be dedicated. I am so proud of her next step, where she will be the inaugural chief diversity officer at the Metropolitan Museum of Art. Her unflinching dedication to our students against endless, harsh criticism will allow her to help reshape the image and core values of one of the world's greatest cultural institutions.

I have also walked hand-in-hand with Mary Coleman, Charles Pryor, Howard Wach, and Bindi Patel. They have been thought partners, and together, we have begun creating a new culture for the Guttman, one that is based in racial equity and educational excellence. I am eternally grateful to them for offering their kindness and companionship to me, and I am thankful our relationships continue to thrive. I am also incredibly grateful for Dr. Nicola Blake, who, like me, has grown up with Guttman and has helped shape its future.

I am beyond blessed to be supported by a wonderful partner, Jared Ragusett, who makes me laugh and lets me sing songs, dance, and take care of our backyard birds. It is in our little world that I find solace and comfort. I am very grateful for loving parents, Chuck and Penny Jordan, who helped me navigate the darkest of times and with whom I enjoy many of life's gifts.

During my time at Guttman, I was graced with great mentors who are also friends. Dr. Tony Picciano, with whom I have coauthored two books, and his wife Elaine Bowden have guided my early career and offered me kind wisdom and love along the way. Drs. Lexa Logue and Colin Chellman are dear research partners and beautiful friends with whom I have shared many joyful moments and rewarding projects. And, to my friend Dr. Vita Rabinowitz, who has always believed in me and who has shared with me tons of encouragement, love, and unconditional support.

To my colleagues at Greenfield Community College, thank you for welcoming me with open arms. I am so happy to be a part of your community and thank each of you for your warmth and generosity.

Lastly, I would like to recognize the people of the City of New York who, since this book was conceived, have experienced unspeakable tragedy and hardship. Much like the City University of New York, which has weathered many impossible storms, the city itself will find its footing, will recover, and will captivate the hearts and minds of the next generation as it has done for generations past.

Preface

In August 2012, I arrived on the steps of the New York Public Library with scores of students, families, faculty, staff, City University of New York (CUNY) administration, and city officials. It was a day of celebration! The New Community College at CUNY was welcoming its inaugural class of students who were gathered between the two great lions, Patience and Fortitude, which flank the grand staircase outside the library. It was my first day of work and the start of a new era for our university. There was a great deal of ceremony, high expectations for the new college, and 289 excited students in colorful shirts that represented their respective learning communities. I had only just begun my teaching career a year prior at Brooklyn College, and the possibility of opening a new college was incredibly exciting. It was the birth of what would become Stella and Charles Guttman Community College.

I often say that Guttman and I grew up together, institution and professor. I started and completed a Ph.D. while I served as a full-time faculty member at the college and helped the institution develop curriculum, policy, and a governance apparatus. My time at Guttman distinctly shaped my understanding of higher education and, particularly, community college students. I have committed myself to serving as an outspoken advocate for my students. I believe that good policy facilitates success and dismantles barriers that continue to promote inequity in outcomes between racial and socioeconomic groups. Guttman has taught me that innovation comes in many forms. At the heart of true innovation is the virtue of honesty. The success of any experiment lies in the scientist's ability to confront failure and make radical change. Honesty is inherent to the process. In turn, successful institutions are ones that use real-time data to address problems and make changes. I am proud to have worked with many colleagues who have remained committed to honesty and navigated the harsh complexities of structural racism that institutions often reproduce.

This book provides one perspective on the evolution of Guttman Community College and the lessons drawn from its origin story and first eight years of operation. There are many Guttman stories. Each of us who participated in its evolution could write a book with similar themes but infused with diverse and radically different experiences. Much of what is written here is a critique rather than an exposition. I believe strongly that institutions mature by actively interrogating mission and vision. I also value data as a core component of an institution's narrative. I have been fortunate to make use of Guttman's early numbers to help tell the story and identify its blind spots. What's under the hood doesn't always look the way we think it should, but it is in the messiness where we find our footing and are able to make change. The critiques made in this book focus on gaps in process and policy. Scores of committed educators worked to plan and implement the Guttman Community College experiment. None of it has been perfect, and we strive to make it better. This book is about the complexities and the lessons of opening a new college in a vast university system and how experimentation was tempered by reality along the way.

This book will describe the evolution of Guttman Community College. The remainder of the introduction will contextualize the birth of Guttman within the postsecondary landscape, providing a historical trajectory both within CUNY and nationally for the reasons why Guttman was engineered in the early years of the 21st century. Chapter 1 will detail the planning stage of the college, describing the methodology for each of the experimental elements of the college, including (1) curriculum, (2) student support, (3) remediation, and (4) workforce preparation. This chapter will navigate the decision-making processes that led to the creation of the *New Community College Concept Paper*, the framework from which the college was fully operationalized. Chapter 2 will discuss the early years of implementation. The faculty and administration quickly realized that the ambitious concept paper was going to be tempered by the constraints of the university system. Much of what was imagined for the college during the planning stage became an impossibility in implementation. Chapter 3 will outline the major challenges the college faced with regard to governance and administration. Without traditional academic departments and academic management, the college's ability to create operational policy was hampered by the flattened structure. This chapter will describe how Guttman developed a governance plan and an administrative apparatus necessary to support a fully functioning college. Chapter 4 will address the curriculum. The innovative curriculum that was marketed as a salve to traditional remediation proved to be costly and labor intensive. Although the concept paper prescribed a sophisticated system of institutional assessment, internal conflict prevented the curriculum from being accurately evaluated. This chapter will speak to the pitfalls and possibilities of innovative community college curricula. Chapter 5 will present the issues facing the college as its first decade in operation comes to a close. Included in this discussion will be an explanation of several ways in which the original model has been altered or is currently under revision. The final chapter of this book will comment on the challenges of the present, including the unanticipated arrival of a global health crisis and subsequent social unrest ahead of the 2020 presidential election. Each chapter will conclude with a section on lessons and implications for the postsecondary system more broadly. These discussions will draw on policies and practices from the Guttman experiment that have been impactful or posed challenges for the college.

Lastly, this book is bound by a story of race and social class. At CUNY and across the country, community colleges serve those students who the meritocratic structures of postsecondary education fail to support. At CUNY, the community colleges are both access points for students of color and barriers to the bachelor's degree. Decades of institutional policy have created a segregated system. Guttman Community College was designed to address inequities in the system but has recognized that these persistent, entrenched gaps in success continue even within a supportive and highly structured model. This book attempts to evaluate why. At the heart of inequality are cultural beliefs about the *other* that privilege the success of some groups and prevent those who are not a part of the majority from accessing valuable capital, social or otherwise. This critique of the Guttman experiment directly confronts these assumptions and explains how damaging broad generalizations about race and social class can be in the project of education. Our students deserve everything we have to give. It is why we are educators.

Foreword

How do you know whether innovations are serving their intended purposes? How does an institution established to innovate and staffed with personnel committed to innovation shift direction when innovations yield unintended consequences? Or when larger forces—social, political, and historical—expose gaps in thinking and planning that were there all along?

Chet Jordan was there at the beginning, when the "New Community College" (subsequently renamed Stella and Charles Guttman Community College), the first community college established in the City University of New York (CUNY) since 1968, opened its doors to students in September 2012. I came to Guttman in April 2017 to take up the provost's position. I was the fourth person in that position in less than five years, a signal I might have heeded more attentively. I arrived with what I thought was a good understanding of how the college worked: a highly structured, learning community-based first-year program; adherence to the "guided pathways" curricular model; intensive, "high-touch" advisement and student services; commitments to a culture of assessment and constructivist pedagogy, educational technology, and experiential learning.

I had been in the CUNY system for 21 years, virtually all of it at two community colleges, Bronx Community College and LaGuardia Community College. I started in the faculty and gradually morphed into an administrator. I spent much of that pre-Guttman time advocating for and working to establish the kinds of reforms on which Guttman was founded.

I knew the rationales for those reforms intimately: abysmal community college graduation rates, the struggles students endured to navigate shifting rules and confusing authorities, and, above all, the expensive and demoralizing trap of long remedial education sequences that preceded accumulation of actual college credits and filled faculty workload hours. A memory stayed with me from my early days at Bronx CC: my department chairperson, a wily character who also chaired the college Curriculum Committee, characterizing a Math Department proposal to tack additional hours onto their zero-credit remedial sequence. "They don't know much," he said of our math colleagues, "but they know how to count." Guttman was created to chart a path toward ending all that, to turn the best research-based thinking about community colleges into institutional reality. I was eager to be part of this great experiment.

Jordan's narrative leads us through the experiment's history, from the first glimmer in then-chancellor Matthew Goldstein's eye, to the extensive planning phase, the bumpy opening years, and through to the present. He brings keen insight to the task, a perspective drawn both from his experience on the ground at Guttman and as a higher education researcher who has probed deeply into CUNY's history. In that sense, Jordan is both an insider and an outsider. The combination yields an institutional history that turns on an urgent and unsettling conclusion and could not be more relevant to the present moment.

My tenure at Guttman has coincided with the college's transition from start-up to adolescence. By 2020, eight years of operation had generated patterns in the data. Though it has since receded from an initial high mark for the first entering class, three-year graduation rates of roughly 40% remain far higher than system and national averages. (Though comparative rates are rising slowly elsewhere as various reforms begin to show results.) We also know now (and did not know until about two years ago) that Guttman graduates struggle after they leave. Their academic performance after transferring to a senior college lags behind other community college graduates. That knowledge has not been easy for faculty to digest. But graduation rates and postgraduate academic standing are not the urgent problems Chet has identified. They are symptoms, not the underlying condition.

Guttman's organizational plan created a first-year curriculum in which every student enters a rigidly structured program in cohorts that move through the freshman year together. Each student was placed in City Seminar, the first-year curriculum centerpiece organized around academic skill development, that required 10.5 hours per week of class time and earned three college credits. Each student, in other words, was presumed to need an additional 7.5 hours of instructional time beyond the conventional 3 hours normally needed to earn 3 credits. In that requirement, in fact, lay the urgent problem that Chet has identified.

Guttman's planners had the best intentions. They scoured the research and consulted the researchers. Placing all students in a 10.5-hour course would allow them to earn 3 college credits while providing the "time on task" and intensive academic support in literacy and quantitative skills instruction the research told them community college students need to be "college ready." But that structure rested on a faulty premise. What if all students did not need extra time? What if this was perpetuating the remedial trap in a different form?

In fact, all students did not need extra time. Over Guttman's first nine years, more than 70% of entering students in each class were assessed by the university as reading and writing proficient. Math proficiency was a different story. Recent research and resulting policy changes have gradually lifted the proportion of Guttman students judged math proficient, rising from a low of 14% in 2014 to 64% in fall 2020. A difference that wide over the course of six years suggests that significant numbers of students never needed additional math "time on task." (It also raises troubling questions about proficiency measures the research has usefully probed.) Here, replicated in a different form, is the remedial quicksand that trapped so many community college students for so long.

Why did the designers of Guttman assume that all students would need so many extra hours of instruction? Why did the research they consulted lead to a variation of the same condition the college was intended to remedy? Why, as Jordan puts it, did "experimentation overshadow the tethers of reality?"

The questions lead back both to the college's founding and out into the wider world. Jordan deftly traces the answer by identifying the racial dynamics that undergird community college education nationally and within the CUNY system. About 67% of students across the seven CUNY community colleges are Black or Latinx. At Guttman, the proportion is 86% today and has never been less than 80%. From the beginning—and predictably so—Guttman has been a minority-serving institution. With that context in place, the planners assumed that all applicants would need to strengthen their reading, writing, and math skills. Why did they arrive at that assumption? And why did the college open and sustain itself on the same assumption despite clear evidence that it was not true?

"We expect that applicants will need to strengthen and expand their skills in reading, writing and math." So reads the executive summary of the *New Community College Concept Paper*, the document that guided Guttman's foundation. Long before the doors opened, the planners applied a deficit logic to the college's prospective students. They would be underprepared, underserved, incapable of college-level work without massive interventions. This conviction shaped the structures, policies, and curriculum Jordan describes in close detail. Most faculty absorbed this belief and signed on ready to follow it. Like the college planners, they did so with the best intentions. But intentions and impact often diverge. Jordan shows how constructing a curriculum in which all students were assigned required seat time far in excess of credits earned; locked in a racialized deficit premise planned, administered, and taught by a largely White staff; and delivered to a mostly Black and Brown student population.

It took me much too long to recognize the impact. Thanks to colleagues like Lavita McMath Turner, Charles Pryor, and Nicola Blake, Black educators passionately committed to making Guttman an authentically equitable institution, I began to grasp what I had inherited and passively accepted. Changing it has been a struggle. We've made some progress—beginning in September 2021, that 10.5-hour class will have been whittled down to 4 hours, and the focus on skill development will be better balanced with academic content. But structural change is only half the battle and perhaps not the hardest half. Very recently, I spoke with a Guttman professor who insisted that the lagging performance of Guttman graduates after transfer can be understood when we accept that without Guttman's nurturing support, many would never have attended, much less graduated from community college. Leaning on our high graduation rates, the professor in effect consigned these students to academic mediocrity and perpetuates the same flawed thinking—an amalgam of paternalism and low expectations—that flowed directly from the concept paper. Guttman is confronting the problem now. Our progress is fitful and stutter-step, but we are moving.

Guttman's dilemma surely mirrors the national racial reckoning for which 2020 will be remembered. As I write in late January 2021, American society has been torn to pieces over four years by a divisive, openly racist president and stunned by a violent anti-democratic insurrection he provoked with incessant lies and appeals to White racial grievance. All this only months after the police murder of George Floyd in Minneapolis catalyzed a massive anti-racist social movement to which Guttman students reacted with grief and fury. In a memorable zoom session in June 2020, they lashed out at all of us—administrators and faculty alike—for failing to meet this awful moment. They demanded that we look at ourselves, our actions, our attitudes, and the college we had made.

Chet Jordan has narrated and dissected the history that brought us to this place. It's an institutional history with a moral twist, told at a moment when structural racism has been, at long last, widely recognized by many White Americans. It's a cautionary tale about half-conscious beliefs and unexamined premises that colonize White educators' minds, permeate institutional actions, and harm students of color despite noble intentions. Future reformers will do well to heed its lessons.

—Dr. Howard M. Wach, Ph.D.

Introduction

In 2007, City University of New York (CUNY) Chancellor Matthew Goldstein unveiled plans to open a new community college. The first new community college at CUNY in over 40 years was imagined as an experiment, one that could radically increase the percentage of students who earned a degree within three years. For decades, community colleges at CUNY and across the country suffered from abysmal completion rates. Chancellor Goldstein seized on an opportunity to serve as the first university system to open a new college using evidence-based research as the framework for both the academic and administrative enterprises. Within five years, CUNY was ready to open Stella and Charles Guttman Community College. The planning team designed a curricular model that supplanted traditional zero-credit remedial courses with an innovative, integrated developmental skills model where students earned credits from the time of matriculation, regardless of their proficiency status. Using a guided pathways blueprint, the framers launched only a select number of programs of study with clear degree pathways to prevent students from wandering aimlessly through majors, accruing excess degree credits, and wasting critical financial aid dollars. Among a number of bold revisions to the standard community college model, Guttman was created without academic departments to promote interdisciplinarity, embedded advising into the curriculum and promoted small class sizes and a highly structured student experience. In a moment of idealism, experimentation overshadowed the tethers of reality. But during the college's first decade of operation, it was forced to reckon with critical missteps that pushed it far from its intended mission.

This book will be framed by both the story of the evolution of a highly experimental community college and the lessons drawn from its planning and implementation that other systems that are engaged in large-scale reform efforts may find useful. Using the Guttman story as a case study, each chapter will detail a component of the college's development and offer a critical assessment of the key successes and challenges that can influence decision-making in other institutions. Guttman was not only an academic experiment, but it also reconstructed the administrative, financial, and advising mechanisms that were long-held traditions in community college education. Conflicts over academic freedom, promotion and tenure, and budget deficits arose as the college reckoned with the realities of working within a large university bureaucracy. These issues circled around the ways in which the academic framework exacerbated the problems it promised to fix, reproduced patterns of structural inequity, and failed to address the true educational demands of the students of color the college enrolled.

On the national stage, Guttman's story speaks to the express need for conscientious reform. The planning team failed to understand the student body before it attempted to apply reforms on a college for which they were unsuited. As the institution engages in a process of self-reflection in order to make the appropriate changes to the curriculum, it is clear that the aspects of the model that were idealized in theoretical research or were successful for different students were mixed at Guttman. This book will focus on the value of deeply understanding institutional context during periods of reform and address complex issues of race and social class as part of the analysis. The Guttman story is not one of successful innovation but rather one where innovation failed to account for the needs of a population.

It was a time of enormous change at CUNY. During the Great Recession, students flocked to CUNY, seeking an inexpensive education to help them enter a fast-changing labor market. This was particularly true of the community colleges where enrollment grew by 44% between 2000 and 2010.[1] Since 2000, the prestige of and admissions standards for the system's four-year colleges rose significantly, prompting many students to use the community colleges as access points to higher education. However, the five community colleges lived up to their promise of access but struggled to move the needle on overall success and completion. In 2007, only 11% of students earned their associate's degree within three years.[2] At first glance, this number is alarming. However, it is important to consider the complicated missions of community colleges and their enormous struggle with providing services to an academically diverse student body. Just as the reputation of the four-year colleges was increasing, new policy mandated all remedial students at CUNY to begin their tenure at one of the community colleges. This was a marked shift from decades of open admissions where remedial students could enroll directly into bachelor's degree programs. Over time, the community colleges became layered with obligations, including remediation, vocational education, transfer preparation, continuing education, and certification. But as fears of continued recession grew larger, there emerged a national consensus that community colleges were underserving the nation's most vulnerable students and had a responsibility to increase their completion rates. And so CUNY responded.

At the time, there was an ethos at the university, one which complimented a nation attempting to recover economically and jump-start the marketplace with fresh ideas and better management. In short, it was a time of *innovation*. Under the direction of Chancellor Matthew Goldstein, CUNY leadership felt that community college education had become stale. Traditional remediation had proven ineffective. Sprawling developmental skills departments ran zero-credit courses with abysmal success rates in reading, writing, and mathematics. Yet any proposed change to remedial education threatened the livelihood of the faculty who staunchly safeguarded their programs. Chancellor Goldstein, however, recognized that CUNY could not continue to ignore the flagging completion rates. In a strategic move, Chancellor Goldstein veered away from demanding wholesale, system-wide reform and instead invested in several experimental programs aimed at improving two-year college completion. The Accelerated Study in Associate Programs (ASAP) initiative launched in 2007. With financial support from the City of New York, ASAP introduced structural supports to full-time community college students on pilot campuses. These supports were designed to ease the burden of attending school full time and nurture the habits necessary to be successful college students. They included transportation subsidies, full financial aid, block scheduling, and intrusive advising. Over 50% of the first ASAP cohort graduated within three years.

Building from the positive results of ASAP, Chancellor Goldstein charged Senior University Dean John Mogulescu with the task of organizing a planning team to design a new community college to incorporate the best reform practices under one roof. In the years that followed, CUNY faculty and administrators embarked on one of the most ambitious projects in the country and one that would have a profound impact on the national postsecondary system. Stella and Charles Guttman Community College made a promise to deliver a high-touch curriculum with an abundance of structural and social-emotional supports primed to increase completion rates. At the center of the mission was a commitment to innovation. From one perspective, Guttman's innovative culture promised to upend traditional higher education silos, eradicating departments in favor of a faculty of the whole. In the same way, the planners promised a flattened administrative structure that minimized characteristically cumbersome bureaucracy that supported most large community colleges. From a strictly academic perspective, though, Guttman pitched itself as the answer to the most challenging quandaries that had plagued community colleges for generations. Through varied modes of curricular overhaul, Guttman placed itself apart from the pack from the outset.

Central to the genesis story of Guttman Community College is a complex discussion of race and socioeconomics that permeate its institutional history. The planning team, led by Dean Mogulescu, was committed to *doing community college differently* and to experimenting with pedagogical and curricular innovations. The desire to strategically innovate, however, overpowered a critical element of the community college story in New York City—the racial background of the students these institutions serve. This book will navigate the difficult topics of structural racism, underscoring how important it is for institutions preparing for periods of reform to deeply understand the student body they plan to serve. The Guttman planning team outlined a well-engineered educational model designed to powerfully increase graduation rates. However, there were key gaps in both the research and design. Critical information about how best to educate an institution composed primarily of students of color was absent from the formative documents and planning. When race and class were mentioned, it was from a deficit perspective. The color-blind approach to progressive postsecondary reform of the early 2000s found fault in remediation but did little to interrogate its roots.

National Context

The first decade of the 21st century was witness to rapid change in the American postsecondary system. For over 200 years, colleges and universities across the country dictated their own policies with very little governmental influence. That all changed when the nation's economic system exited the industrial period and arrived in a postindustrial world commanded by the knowledge and service sectors. This shock to the system, coupled with a global economic downturn, propelled a demand for college degrees like no other period had since the aftermath of World War II. Yet the higher education system people clamored to get into remained firmly meritocratic and extraordinarily expensive. By 2012, the national student debt totaled $1.1 billion with 10% of loans at least 90 days delinquent.[3] But for many, the investment was crucial to their future livelihoods. The once expansive middle-wage economy rapidly vanished, leaving the least-educated workers four times more likely than college-educated individuals to be unemployed.[4]

For many students and their families, the most reasonable and accessible option was to enroll at one of the nation's community colleges.

Community colleges have long provided varied types of education in the locales they served. They offer programs ranging from academic to highly vocational and technical and traditionally conferred associate's degrees and certificates to graduates. Two-year colleges, particularly those in large university systems, also enroll a diverse student body in terms of race, socioeconomic status, and academic preparation. Just before the economic downturn, 44% of Black and 51% of Hispanic college-going students attended a two-year public college.[5] Community colleges disproportionately enrolled remedial students in comparison to four-year colleges. At the start of the 21st century, 23% of entering community college freshmen required remediation in writing, while 35% were identified as remedial in math.[6] During the recession, the community college sector expanded by over 20%.[7] In turn, the number of students of color and the proportion of remedial student community colleges served rapidly increased.

As demand increased, there was a clear recognition that if community colleges were to serve as an economic engine for the sputtering American economy, outcomes had to markedly improve. In 2010, only 39% of community college students had earned an associate's degree within six years. Not surprisingly, the success rates are widely varied by race. Within six years, 67% of White community college students had earned a degree compared to 49% of Hispanic and 41% of Black students.[8] At some colleges and universities, these numbers were far lower. These persistently low outcomes can be attributed to a number of issues germane to community colleges. First, in 2005, only 40% of community college students enrolled full time.[9] A large majority of students enroll at community college to brush up on skills for a job, to earn baseline credits in order to transfer to a four-year college, or to complete remedial courses. Low completion rates are often the result of the mixed mission of the sector itself. Second, the ways in which remedial courses were traditionally offered created barriers to student success. During the latter half of the 20th century, zero-credit courses became the traditional mode of delivering basic skills in reading, writing, and math. In 2005, over 40% of community college students reported having taken at least one remedial course.[10] Recent research, however, signals that one-third to one-quarter of the students who have historically been assigned to remediation would have done well in college-level work had they been afforded the opportunity.[11] Third, community colleges enroll more non-traditional, low-income, students of color than does the four-year college sector. There persist, however, disparities in outcomes by race and socioeconomic status. Six-year completion outcomes point to race as a leading factor in community college student dropout. For example,

56% of Black students dropped out of college within six years compared to 44% of Hispanic and 41% of White students. Furthermore, only 18% of Black students earned a degree compared to 24% of Hispanic and 30% of White students.[12] Although community colleges promote missions of access and opportunity, sector outcomes consistently indicate cycles of institutional racism and poverty.

Emphasis on community college outcomes was further accelerated by President Barack Obama's administration. The White House seized on an opportunity to develop a skilled workforce to lift up the stagnant economy. President Obama set two national goals to be achieved by 2020: (1) have the highest number of college graduates in the world and (2) community colleges will graduate five million new graduates. The autonomy of the community college sector gave way to the desires of the president. In October 2016, the White House announced five strategic goals for the nation's two-year colleges:

1. Collaborate with local businesses to establish workforce partnerships
2. Create partnerships with four-year colleges to ease transfer process
3. Teach developmental skills
4. Support students' needs
5. Develop online course offerings[13]

The federal government funded competitive grant programs to influence community colleges to raise completion rates and bolster their academic programs. In addition to governmental interest in community colleges, private philanthropic groups like the Bill & Melinda Gates Foundation saw an opportunity to influence national policy by contributing large sums of donor money to community college reform.

Foundations like Gates, Lumina, and Robin Hood were leaders in the two-year college completion agenda throughout the recession and postrecession era. The Gates Foundation, for example, launched the $34.8 million Completion by Design program in 2010 to significantly raise the community college completion rates within five years. The program identified colleges in nine target states that served as incubators of research for best practices in curricular and student support overhaul.[14] The rationale for such significant investment was deeply connected to what was perceived of as a potential shortage of low- to mid-wage workers. In fact, the Gates Foundation noted that without significant investment in degree completion, there would be a pronounced shortage in the workforce across many employment sectors.[15] From a philanthropic perspective, investment in community college completion was intimately connected to the advancement of a policy agenda that directed students into a range of technical and highly profitable careers. At a time when public funding for higher education was waning, particularly in the community college sector, the possibility of recouping losses by way of private donor funding was an attractive option for community college leaders. However, the proposition of funding came with a range of requisite institutional and academic overhauls. In many ways, the recession period in the United States pushed community colleges to think like businesses. In order to acquire federal and private funding, two-year institutions were required to establish institutional goals and practices in areas of (1) technology, (2) learning outcomes assessment, (3) innovative pedagogy, and (4) streamlined student services.

The Community College Research Center (CCRC) provided a wealth of research that supported such reforms. The CCRC explained that, at the institutional level, five principles were essential to ensuring growth in student completion:

1. Set learning outcomes and completion goals
2. Measure student learning and progress
3. Identify learning and achievement gaps
4. Align practices and policies to improve outcomes
5. Evaluate and improve alignment effectiveness[16]

At the heart of these principles was a mandate of organizational efficiency and continuous evaluation of student outcomes data. This approach marked a significant cultural shift for community colleges, which had, for decades, operated on a mission of access and enrollment numbers to justify taxpayer funding. It was, in effect, a move toward strict accountability with the central metric of focus being substantially increased completion rates. Private philanthropists tied multimillion-dollar funding opportunities to reforms that they believed could directly impact the national economy. Many of the calls for proposals spoke to a need for a swift break from the traditional academic silos and a shift toward experiential, problem-based learning that might better position students to enter the workforce with the skills to be active members of innovative teams. It was a new era of vocational education by a different name.

The major collegiate organizations promptly responded to the call for reform. The American Association of Colleges and Universities (AAC&U), for example, generated a detailed compilation of student learning outcomes applicable to all 21st-century college students. Alongside these learning outcomes that addressed such skills as information literacy, civic knowledge, teamwork and problem solving, and quantitative literacy, the AAC&U encouraged colleges to integrate a series of high-impact practices (HIPS) into their curricula.[17] These HIPS included first-year seminars, service learning, and ePortfolios to showcase student learning. These efforts intended to restructure the traditional community college curriculum toward an outcomes-driven design connected directly to the types of qualities reformers believed attractive to employers.

At the same time that colleges were engaged in a sustained period of educational and structural reform, two-year institutions were seeing incredible sector growth for which Black and Hispanic students were largely responsible. In 1993, there were 728,000 Hispanic students between the ages of 18–24 enrolled in college across the country. By 2012, that number had grown to 2.4 million.[18] The overwhelming majority of these students enrolled in community colleges, lacking the educational record or financial capability needed to compete for baccalaureate admission. As many more students of color enrolled in associate's programs, they were met with academic and bureaucratic barriers that made degree attainment and transfer into baccalaureate programs unattainable for many. For thousands of students, zero-credit remediation prevented them from accruing credits in a timely manner, especially as critical financial aid dollars dwindled each semester. As educators raced to design flashy curricula that promised to reinvigorate the labor market with employable associate's degree holders, the reforms did little to raise completion rates. Certainly, there were examples of modest gains, but the large leaps the country sought were far from ubiquitous.

CUNY

The CUNY faced the same challenges, if not more dire, than the rest of the country with regard to community college completion. Over two-thirds of each entering community college class required some form of basic skills remediation. Only 30% of students who enrolled in developmental math completed the required sequence. This revolving door of remedial students was the chief contributor to high attrition rates and low degree attainment. For generations, exams given at the time of entry determined whether students were placed into zero-credit remedial courses. Exams in reading, writing, and math had strict cutoff scores with little opportunity to test again prior to matriculation. Prior to 2000, remedial students could still apply to and enroll in any of the university's four-year colleges. However, in response to political criticism citing low academic rigor and abysmal graduation rates, newly appointed chancellor Matthew Goldstein advanced a plan to restrict remedial programs to the community colleges. In part, this was an effort by Chancellor Goldstein to resurrect the prestige of the CUNY four-year colleges that had been marred by scandal and decreased legislative investment in recent years. There were, however, a host of unintended consequences that confronted the university in the decade following the shift in remedial policy. Paramount among these was the demographic split between the two- and four-year colleges caused by the elimination of remediation in baccalaureate programs. At CUNY, and across the country, the vast majority of students enrolled in remedial education are students of color. CUNY's decision to enroll all remedial students at the community colleges meant that the two-year colleges overenrolled students of color. In turn, the four-year colleges became Whiter and wealthier.

During the first decade of the 21st century, the CUNY community colleges became the site of contradictory policy initiatives. In order to raise the national standing of the four-year institutions, the community colleges took on all of CUNY's remedial students. Years of remedial education proved that most of the students who enrolled in these course sequences ultimately dropped out. During the recession, though, national attention was paid to increasing community college completion rates. The university recognized that it was forced to reckon with a problem it had created. Chancellor Goldstein often tells a story that he woke up in the middle of the night sometime in 2007 and was walking around his apartment trying to figure out how to fix the community colleges. He believed that students were dropping out because they entered college with inadequate support necessary to succeed. After his sleepless night, he commissioned Senior University Dean John Mogulescu to organize a team in his collaborative programs office to find structural remedies that could assist in promoting completion. Dean Mogulescu's staff of researchers and university professionals put forward a plan for the ASAP initiative. The ASAP program provided students with the structural support they needed to graduate on time from a community college. This support included (1) New York City transportation funds, (2) block scheduling, (3) proactive advising, and (4) free textbooks. Over 50% of the first ASAP cohort graduated within three years. Since its inception, ASAP has grown exponentially and continues to show positive completion outcomes.

ASAP quickly became a point of pride for CUNY and the nation. In 2015, President Obama's White House singled out ASAP as an example of the possibilities of building *high-quality* community colleges.[19] At CUNY, though, ASAP existed as a program within a highly complex and, at times, ideologically entrenched university. Across all sectors, the academic departments had long been the standard-bearers of the educational enterprise. At the community colleges, developmental education programs thrived with a steady flow of students to support scores of class sections each semester. Although remediation was recognized as one of the most critical causes of community college attrition, there was little appetite for wholesale reform from the faculty who taught in those departments. Recognizing that sweeping change was an impossibility, Dean Mogulescu and his team engineered ASAP to fit within the current educational framework. In its early years, ASAP limited the number of remedial students it enrolled. As the program grew and provided access to thousands of additional students, ASAP enrolled remedial students and relied on its well-tested and ever-evolving advising mechanism to ensure that any student who did require developmental education completed those courses quickly and with the proper academic support. An analysis of recent ASAP cohorts shows that 46.6% of students who enter with at least one developmental need graduate within three years compared to 22.4%of students who are not enrolled in ASAP.[20] Early criticism that ASAP prevented remedial students from accessing its important services has long since been quelled. These data indicate that enhanced services that contribute to overall student success are beneficial for a diverse population of students. As ASAP's outcomes outshined any other recent attempts at community college reform, Chancellor Goldstein's administration seized on the possibility of scaling its operations.

Adjacent to ASAP's formation was the creation of another program that promised to provide efficient developmental education to students for a fraction of the cost of tuition. In 2009, CUNY completed the development and implementation of the CUNY Start program. CUNY Start restructured the remedial experience into an intensive one-semester sequence of basic skills development. Rather than initiating the financial aid process to enroll in zero-credit, matriculated remedial courses, CUNY Start positioned itself as a prematriculation program and charged students only $75 to enroll. In addition to the low cost, CUNY Start overhauled the curriculum and pedagogical approach to remediation. CUNY Start developed semester-long course material in English and math that drew on best practices of the period of postsecondary innovation that dominated the early 2000s. Moving away from lecture-based instruction, courses in CUNY Start adhered to a student-centered approach to teaching, using real-world problems to stimulate active conversation of concepts in the classroom.[21] CUNY Start has exhibited promising outcomes. A recent study indicates that 57% of CUNY Start students demonstrated college readiness by the end of the program semester in comparison to 25% of the control group. Furthermore, CUNY Start students outpaced their control group peers by eight percentage points in reading and nine in writing.[22] The report underscores that while there is an initial delay in credit accumulation as students defer matriculation to participate in CUNY Start, they are predicted to catch up to control group students in credits earned by the fourth post-program semester. Much like ASAP, CUNY Start operates outside of the traditional academic infrastructure. Because of its programmatic status, administrators and teachers in the program have been free to experiment with pedagogy and set expectations that would have otherwise been blocked by departmental faculty.

It was within this matrix of experimental reforms that the idea for a new community college was formed. Planning began in earnest in 2007 under the direction of Dean Mogulescu. In 2008, Director of Collaborative Programs Tracy Meade went on leave from her position to spearhead the planning process. In part, what would become the New Community College (NCC) at CUNY (later Guttman) was a marriage of ASAP and CUNY Start. The planning team coupled the structural supports that had generated positive outcomes in ASAP with many of the student-centered pedagogies of CUNY Start. The central mission of the NCC was to substantially increase community college graduation rates. The boundaries for Meade and Mogulescu to do so were limitless. With abundant funding promised by Chancellor Goldstein and the CUNY central office, the planning of the NCC was an exercise in imaginative thinking. Faculty, staff, and administrators from across the university and the nation participated in a dialogue about how the new college would operate and what the principles of education might be. Surveys were distributed, working groups formed, and founding faculty were hired to develop curricula. It was to be the first new college at CUNY in over four decades, and the stakes for its success were enormously high. The institution had to demonstrate that it was capable of restructuring the traditional community college experience in order to maintain its unique place in the university's landscape. Furthermore, the national postsecondary community was watching to see if CUNY could actually alter the persistent inequities community college students had historically faced in outcomes, graduation, transfer, and baccalaureate attainment. Along with the great energy around the formation of the college, there was an equal amount of criticism well before the institution opened in 2012. As this book will detail, there were deep concerns about the rigor of the proposed curriculum, the college governance plan, academic freedom, and financial feasibility and sustainability. It was unclear if the new model could realistically be scaled to meet the needs of several thousand students or if it would remain a boutique institution serving only a few hundred. Early questions would find their answers in the first decade of operation.

The opening of a new college is almost always cause for joy and speculation. This book will chronicle the evolution of Guttman Community College at the CUNY. In so doing, it will speak to the myriad lessons that can be valuable for a higher education landscape that is hungry for innovation and reform. After a decade in operation, Guttman Community College is confronting the specters of its past as it attempts to address the blind spots of the planning team and the complex assumptions about the student population that were baked into the educational model. Each chapter of this book will conclude with a section focused on how the Guttman experience can provide lessons for higher education reform. As the college continues to revise its infrastructure and prepares to enroll additional students, its historical narrative offers important insight into areas of racial inequity, leadership, innovative education, and data-driven decision-making. Each subsequent chapter details a segment of the institution's development and navigates the early story of CUNY's newest community college.

Notes

1. The CUNY Office of Institutional Research and Assessment, *CUNY Enrollment Trends: Fall 1950–2010* (New York, NY: The CUNY Office of Institutional Research and Assessment, 2016).
2. The CUNY Office of Institutional Research and Assessment, *System Retention and Graduation Rates of Full-Time First-Time Freshmen in Associate Programs by Year of Entry: Total University* (New York, NY: The CUNY Office of Institutional Research and Assessment, 2008).
3. Sara Goldrick-Rab, *The Color of Student Debt: Implications of Federal Loan Program Reforms for Black Students and Historically Black Colleges and Universities* (Madison, WI: Wisconsin Hope Lab, 2014), 2.
4. Lauren Schudde and Sara Goldrick-Rab, "On Second Chances and Stratification: How Sociologists Think about Community Colleges," *Community College Review* 43, no. 1 (2014): 27–45.
5. Ford Foundation, *What We Know About Community College Low-Income and Minority Student Outcomes: Descriptive Statistics from National Surveys* (Washington, DC: Ford Foundation, 2005), 14.
6. Ford Foundation, 37.
7. American Association of Community Colleges, *Community College Enrollment Crisis? Historical Trends in Community College Enrollment* (Washington, DC: American Association of Community Colleges, 2019), 4.
8. Elissa Nadworthy, "College Completion Rates Are Up but the Numbers Will Still Surprise You," *NPR*, www.npr.org/2019/03/13/681621047/college-completion-rates-are-up-but-the-numbers-will-still-surprise-you.
9. American Association of Community Colleges, 4.
10. Brookings Institute, *Evidence-Based Reforms in College Remediation Are Gaining Steam—and so Far Living Up to the Hype* (Washington, DC: Brookings Institute, 2018).
11. Brookings Institute.
12. National Student Clearinghouse, *Completing College: A National View of Student Attainment Rates by Race and Ethnicity-Fall 2010 Cohort* (Herndon, VA: National Student Clearinghouse, 2017), 16.

13. The White House, *Building American Skills Through Community Colleges* (Washington, DC: The White House, 2016), 1.
14. Bill & Melinda Gates Foundation, *Foundation Launches $35 Million Program to Help Boost Community College Graduation Rates* (Seattle, WA: Bill & Melinda Gates Foundation, 2010).
15. Bill & Melinda Gates Foundation.
16. Davis Jenkins, *Redesigning Community Colleges for Completion: Lessons from Research on High-Performance Organizations*, CCRC Working Paper No. 24 (New York, NY: Columbia University, Teachers College, Community College Research Center, 2011).
17. "Inquiry and Analysis VALUE Rubric" (Association of American Colleges and Universities, 2009), www.aacu.org/value/rubrics/inquiry-analysis.
18. Pew Research Center, *More Hispanics, Blacks Enrolling in College, but Lag in Bachelor's Degrees* (Washington, DC: Pew Research Center, 2014).
19. The White House, "White House Unveils America's College Promise Proposal: Tuition-Free Community College for Responsible Students," *News Release*, January 9, 2015.
20. Diana Strumbos, Donna Linderman, and Carson Hicks, "Postsecondary Pathways Out of Poverty: City University of New York Accelerated Study in Associate Programs and the Case for National Policy," *The Russel Sage Foundation Journal of Social Sciences* 4, no. 3 (2018): 100–117.
21. MDRC, *Becoming College-Ready: Early Findings from a CUNY Start Evaluation* (New York, NY: MDRC, 2018).
22. MDRC.

1 The Planning Stage

Origin Story

In fall 2007, Dean Mogulescu met with Chancellor Goldstein to discuss how to proceed with a grant application that proposed a pilot program for restructuring first-year courses in the community college sector at CUNY. The chancellor, however, was not at all interested in a pilot program but proposed that a new community college be developed as an incubator for reform with the singular mission of raising completion rates. Dean Mogulescu drew from his 30 years at CUNY, 23 of those in the central office, and a team of educators in the collaborative programs wing of his operation to begin the brainstorm for a new community college. Much of the work was prefaced by years of investment in precollege programs like the CUNY Language Immersion Program, CUNY Prep Transitional High School, and a number of adult literacy and GED programs. Dean Mogulescu recruited long-time CUNY veteran John Garvey and colleague Tracy Meade, who would eventually head the planning team, to serve as the core leaders for the project.[1]

Once Dean Mogulescu organized his senior staff, they went about the job of crafting a message for why a new community college at CUNY was necessary. Early conversations attempted to steer clear of additional space as a rationale for the new institution that was intended to serve a small fraction of what the other community colleges enrolled. Chancellor Goldstein wanted the new college to be a model for what was possible, which implied that its development would speak directly to the flaws in the current system. Mogulescu and Meade rightly recognized that there would be a good deal of criticism from stalwart community college faculty and administrators who believed the model of access far outweighed the need for high graduation rates. One common rationale for low completion numbers across the country was that community college students enrolled for many reasons and many never intended to complete an associate's degree. While that is certainly true for some students, there are also critical barriers to success that deter students who want to graduate from completing their coursework. New York City and its university system were, however, shifting toward a new reality where some college experience, and even the associate's degree, were not competitive on the job market. Unlike many areas of the country where community colleges provided direct access to local industry, the CUNY community colleges had, since 2000, become sites of transfer. In 2007, though, when the planning phase of the new college began, there was still a strong belief that associate's degree holders could provide a critical mass for a potential gap in the labor market. Ultimately, this belief was determined to be unfounded.

As the planning team continued to garner support and deflect opposition across the university, Tracy Meade and her team began work on what would be the blueprint for the new college. Much of this chapter will be dedicated to the development of the *New Community College Concept Paper*. Beginning in 2007 and continuing through August 2008, the planning team attempted to identify what Dean Mogulescu referred to as "trouble spots" in the community college experience—places where students typically struggled in the first year. Once the concept paper was finished, it was widely distributed for feedback. This chapter will discuss the various forms of critical feedback the planning team received about their radical revision to the community college experience.

A New Community College Concept Paper

Beginning in February 2008, Tracy Meade led a team in drafting *A New Community College Concept Paper*. For six months prior, the planning team solicited input from national postsecondary experts for the foundational components of the innovative educational model. In writing the concept paper, the planning team relied on individuals like Dr. Thomas Bailey who was, at the time, head of the CCRC at Columbia University. Other luminaries like W. Norton Grubb at UC Berkeley, Melissa Roderick at the University of Chicago, and Randy Bass at Georgetown comprised the college's first advisory board. As researchers from research institutions, these individuals relied on empirical evidence and popular scholarly literature to offer opinions on how the new college should be constructed. Prior to writing the concept paper, the planning team did consult a number of CUNY staff members. Most of these individuals, however, served in roles as senior administrators on the campuses and in the central office. It is not at all surprising, then, that the concept paper emerges from various streams of scholarship and is supported less by the realities of a community college education within the context and environment of CUNY but rather within the reform ideology of the decade.

Between February and August 2008, the planning team constructed a vision of the new community college from expert research. In its first pages, the concept paper outlines the rationale for a new community college. Chancellor Goldstein identified raising completion rates as the institution's central mission.[2] From the outset, the planning team remarks that although the concept paper attempts to dismantle barriers that have long plagued community college students in their path toward completion, it was not intended to be a singular approach to raising graduation rates but instead as one possible pathway for reform. Additionally, the tone of the document intended to separate itself from the traditional community college paradigm. It noted that the roles of faculty and staff would be markedly different at the new college, resulting in altered expectations and institutional policies.[3] The first departure from the normal community college experience was that of mandatory full-time enrollment. Although approximately 80% of community college students enroll full time in the first semester, many drop to part time rather quickly, slowing time-to-degree. In conjunction with full-time enrollment, the planning team intimated that the additional time in the classroom would afford students the opportunity to build an academic foundation *beyond proficiency* rather than spending time attempting to complete layers of zero-credit remediation.[4] Lastly, it was proposed that the college operate under a guided pathways model, limiting the number of degree programs and course options to generate a more efficient and predictable trajectory toward completion.

The concept paper advanced an admissions process that served the dual function of college preparatory and educational advising. Recognizing the value of relationship building as a critical component of student retention, the planning team imagined an admissions process that invited students to campus on several occasions to ensure their understanding of the institution's unique structure and requirements.[5] On many campuses, student services are often detached from one another, and in some cases, they are in separate locations on the grounds. The planners for the new college recommended that admissions, financial aid, and the bursar be co-located, providing a one-stop hub in the geographical center of the institution. The expanded definition and responsibilities of the admissions office included partnering with faculty to administer diagnostic assessments to students. The planning team believed that the traditional apparatus, placement examinations, be abandoned in favor of a more holistic approach to developmental skills evaluation. Since the new college planned to eliminate zero-credit remediation, a topic that will be discussed in further detail later in this chapter, the diagnostic assessments were not used for placement but rather to give faculty a clearer understanding of the kinds of skills students were entering with.[6]

Under Tracy Meade's direction, the planning team prepared a complex educational model for the new community college. The academic enterprise was founded within a set of pedagogical and structural principles, most of which were drawn from external research. First, the concept paper called for the elimination of zero-credit remediation.[7] The planning team believed that in order for students to gain momentum toward graduation, they had to immediately begin college earning credits. The concept paper advanced an integrative developmental education model where students would spend more time in the classroom, honing their basic skills in reading, writing, and math while also engaging with college-level content.[8] Although the move to eliminate zero-credit remediation was heralded as a significant positive departure from the traditional community college model, the planning team instead recommended a college structure born of the belief that *all* students who enrolled would require remediation. This approach emerged from the work of James Slevin, a former department chair at Georgetown University. Slevin opined that all introductory college courses should be "radically remedial."[9] Slevin, however, was speaking from a context far removed from CUNY. At CUNY, remediation was primarily a space populated by low-income, students of color, resulting from disinvestment in public secondary education and heightened admissions standards. Together, these factors created a critical barrier to baccalaureate access. Unlike Slevin's definition of remediation that might better have been labeled as foundational, remediation at CUNY was largely a practice of racial sorting.

The planning team invested significant time in developing the required first-year curriculum. The features of the first-year core curriculum included

- the restructuring of semesters into shorter modules;
- the incorporation of student development and workplace education into the curriculum;
- full-scale implementation of learning communities.[10]

Central to the first-year core was the two-semester course called City Seminar. City Seminar was intended to serve as the space in which students received their developmental skills remediation while earning college course credit. The course was to be divided into modules in which students investigated a series of case studies related to a public issue in New York City. Credit was to be awarded on a sliding scale at the completion of each module, after approximately seven weeks. Students who made adequate progress during the first module advanced into the next component while students who had not earned credit continued to work on the requisite skills in the next session. This approach called for four faculty members to teach each of the course components (reading and writing, quantitative reasoning, a case study section, and a supplemental instructional space). Each component addressed basic developmental skills using the case study as the source from which student work was derived. Group Workspace, the supplemental instructional component, initially was conceived to be a dual-purpose space for individual and group advising and additional time for students to work on projects.[11]

The first-year core curriculum also included a Professional Studies course, one that was meant to link students to local employers and introduce them to the skills necessary to thrive in workplace culture. The concept paper, however, took employment at face value and assumed a meritocratic approach would ultimately lead students to gainful employment. The Professional Studies course, which was later titled Ethnographies of Work, was designed with the assumption that many of the new college's students would be entering the workforce with their associate's degree, a presumption that was quickly negated by the demand for baccalaureate transfer by the time the college opened. In addition to the Professional Studies course, the concept paper included in the educational model a Math Topics course for which students would spend 200% more time on task in math than they would in a traditional college.[12] Recognizing the high failure rate in remedial math courses, the planning team offered a substantial increase in the time on task as a potential remedy. All students, regardless of proficiency upon entry, would be required to enroll in 135 contact hours of math in the first semester.

In 2008, the planning team imagined 12 majors for the college. They included the following:

- Nursing
- Surgical technology
- Environmental technology
- Energy services management
- Earth and environmental sciences
- Information studies
- Geographic information systems
- Supply chain management
- Community health worker
- Disability studies
- Urban education
- Urban studies

When the college opened, however, most of these initial proposals for degree programs had been scrapped. Because of space constraints for the new college and feedback regarding the scalability of the large number and highly technical foci of many of the majors, the planners settled on six degree programs: (1) liberal arts and sciences, (2) urban studies, (3) information technology, (4) business, (5) human services, and (6) health information technology. The second and subsequent years of a student's time at the new college were initially tailored to the potential for employment postgraduation or, in some cases, for students to enroll in joint degree programs in preparation for transfer. The concept paper indicated that the majors were to be interdisciplinary and focused on horizontal skill-building that was perceived to be a demand of the new knowledge economy.[13] To this end, students in the majors were poised to engage with fieldwork, internships, and a continued focus on reading and writing skills. An Office of Partnerships was imagined as a way to forge the workforce connections necessary to sustain such a career-centric curriculum. This office was designed to be a multifaceted hub of job placement information and direct access to local employers to support classroom and internship work. The planning team also called for strong joint articulation agreements with CUNY baccalaureate programs. These agreements would allow students to identify a bachelor's degree pathway from the time of entry and work with advising staff to complete the necessary components of the transfer application. The document states that after graduation, "every effort [would] be taken to help students transfer to CUNY and other colleges in cohorts."[14] By the time the college opened in 2012, however, these articulations did not exist.

In conjunction with the highly innovative academic model, the concept paper outlined a comprehensive set of student support services designed to promote retention and completion. It was clear by 2007 when the planning started for the new college that advising was critical to student success. Initially, the Group Workspace component of City Seminar was named as the advising site in the first-year experience (FYE). It was assumed at the start of the planning phase that faculty teaching in City Seminar would also serve as student advisors. In fact, the concept paper signaled that faculty would hold small-group and individual advising sessions on a weekly basis with additional support from professional advisors.[15] When the college opened, however, professional advisors took primary responsibility for student support services, with faculty having no principal role in advising. Other services that were planned for the college included a robust set of student activities to provide relational opportunities for commuter students and networks for employment and external services. The planning team assumed that students enrolling at the college would be faced with a host of challenges, including chronic health problems, housing, employment, and childcare.[16] Much like the rationale for intensive remediation, the rationale for providing extensive services to the new college's students emerged from presumptions about race that were uniformly applied to the entire population.

Lastly, the concept paper called for a high-tech learning environment. At the center of a range of technological solutions, the planners recommended that students and faculty alike develop robust ePortfolios. Electronic portfolios were, at the time, a fashionable educational tool to showcase and illustrate an archive of work. Although there was some modest evidence of impact on student outcomes, interest in such portfolios has largely faded on the national stage. However, the planners saw an opportunity for technology, and especially ePortfolios, to serve as critical extensions of classroom work and student/faculty and peer collaboration. Not only would discussion boards and online communities permit students to stay in close contact with one another outside the classroom but also ePortfolios could easily serve as repositories for work so that students could bridge interdisciplinary connections between courses and develop a longitudinal archive of achievements.[17] The new college was able to secure a significant investment in technology by the time it opened in 2012. Although the ambitious ideal of integrated connectivity was tempered by the realities of space and use, the college has certainly made use of hardware and software that has not yet been fully operationalized on other campuses.

Critical Assessment of the Concept Paper

Once the concept paper was completed, the planning team released it to a range of stakeholders for feedback. Dean Mogulescu and Tracy Meade met with key governing bodies from across the university to solicit comment. Almost immediately, however, there was criticism of both the content and the process. Beginning in early November 2008, planning team leadership visited each of the community colleges, the University Faculty Senate, and members of the central office. Although the community colleges recognized issues of retention and graduation as central problems facing the sector, participants in the dialogue with the planning team expressed dissatisfaction with the opening of a new institution when they believed resources should go to existing colleges struggling to uplift student outcomes. It was apparent in several of the comments that the tone of the concept paper suggested that community colleges had failed to serve students effectively. If the concept paper was considered an "indictment," of, as one respondent stated, current community college policy and practice, it also solidified what many members of the community college sector said about their students—that their complicated lives were to blame for their inability to complete their course of study. As much critique came from the faculty regarding the tenor of the paper, the planning team and the instructional staff placed blame on externalities rather than on the barriers constructed by the postsecondary system itself. In one case, a respondent from a community college stated that the secondary system was to blame and fixing it was someone else's problem, not CUNY's, while another individual from the same college argued that young community college students dropped out because life events happened that force them out of school.

The University Faculty Senate was a principal critic of the new college throughout its planning phase. The commentary from the Executive Committee of the Senate in 2008 focused on issues of governance, planning, and operation. First, they suggested that the learning community model, though novel, was extreme and believed that negative student behaviors could emerge as a result of the forced time together in a series of yearlong classes. Another rebuke of the educational model came by way of comparison of the college to a 13th year of high school with incredibly low standards that planned to offer experiences rather than courses. Much like several members of the community college faculty, some senators argued that the new college was an exercise in experimentation and did not consider the lived experiences of the students it would ultimately enroll. Several months later, in February 2009, Dean Mogulescu and Tracy Meade met with the community college caucus of the University Faculty Senate.[18] The various representatives from the community colleges questioned Dean Mogulescu on why the planning team identified community college teaching, particularly in the area of remediation, as the source of the problem. They further indicated that if they had sustained financial and logistical resources on their campuses, a new college would not be necessary to solve completion issues. One member of the caucus noted that ASAP had demonstrated substantial gains in student outcomes without modifying the curriculum and asked why resources could not be aligned to existing structures. Toward the end of what became a tense and critical conversation about the concept paper, Dean Mogulescu defended his record stating, "My whole life at CUNY has been in service of disadvantaged students. . . . I'm not the person some of you think I am."[19] The debate ended with a comment from one member in response to Dean Mogulescu: "We have a commitment too, have worked as experts in developmental education for decades. . . . I have a Ph.D. and didn't see our expertise reflected in the NCC bibliography. Insulting."[20]

In a very different tone, senior members of the university community and the new college's advisory board praised the model and offered considerable feedback to the planning team. Kingsborough Community College president Regina Peruggi lauded the bold steps taken by the planning team. She remarked that "the new community college takes an absolutely refreshing approach to remediation" and that the design incorporated all of the best practices necessary to ensure positive student outcomes."[21] LaGuardia Community College president Gail Mellow remarked that "if enacted, the groundbreaking initiative would propel CUNY to become a national epicenter for educational innovation in community colleges."[22] Throughout comments made by the college's first advisory board, many lauded the bold vision but at the same time attempted to prepare the planning team for the challenges of operational realities. Melissa Roderick, professor of social service administration at the University of Chicago, challenged the planning team to carefully think about their intended student body. She acknowledged that the new model might very well be attractive to Hispanic students interested in higher education but that the college should not suspect that these students, in any way, be low performing as the concept paper suggests. Dr. Roderick further argues that although students would benefit from a structured FYE, it also needed to consider how to educate students who were widely varied in terms of academic experience.[23]

David Crook, University Dean for Institutional Research and Assessment, called the proposal "revolutionary" and "exhilarating." Crook, one of CUNY's best critical minds and sharpest policy experts, posed a number of questions to the planning team regarding the fiscal and logistical feasibility of some of what was planned. The concept paper called for a robust enterprise of professional staff to support the wide range of student services. Dean Crook suggested that the admissions process that called for one-to-one interviews be reconsidered within the context of CUNY's limited resources, especially as the college planned for enrollment growth. In contrast, however, Dean Crook commented that the student services section of the concept paper was underdeveloped. He reasoned that the planning team ascribed much of the responsibility of low completion primarily to subpar academic preparation. Crook cited recent studies that indicated extra-institutional factors, notably those related to a student's finances, substantially contributed to the dropout rate. In concert with Roderick and others, Dean Crook indicated that the one-size-fits-all approach, particularly to remediation, that framed the FYE, could prevent high-performing students from engaging with challenging coursework. He also cautioned the planning team to reconsider heavy emphasis on workforce preparedness and job placement, signaling that many students already have jobs and may not be interested in tapping into that component of the model.[24]

Overall, opinions about the new college were celebratory, critical, and cautionary. Voices of praise typically came from researchers, especially those whose work was cited in the concept paper, who viewed the college as an experimental opportunity that could potentially serve as a data incubator on policy reform efforts. Critical feedback primarily emerged from the CUNY faculty ranks. Although national criticism of the college would come later down the road as the institution prepared to open, initial objection to the planning team's processes and design principles laid the groundwork for subsequent, more vocal opposition. A number of individuals expressed optimism in the possibility of reforming the traditional community college paradigm yet tempered their enthusiasm with a more pragmatic understanding of issues of fiscal planning, operational limitations, and bureaucratic barriers. Over the next several years ahead of the college's opening, significant modifications would be made to the framework laid out in the concept paper. However, the issue of the one-size-fits-all educational model was left largely untouched, an omission that paved the way for challenging racial dynamics at the new college.

Lessons for Higher Education

Perspectives in Planning

One significant lesson to be drawn from the planning stage is how insular the planning team was as it designed the concept paper. Dean Mogulescu's team operated outside of traditional university governance and reported to the central administration rather than to the campuses and their faculties. This allowed his team to largely work in isolation from bodies that would ordinarily be responsible for the oversight of such areas of the academic enterprise as curriculum design. The new community college project was unique in the sense that it originated in the central office which then shifted authority for its inception to a remote group of administrators in Mogulescu's collaborative programs division. The conceptual framing of the college, which was evidenced in the concept paper, proceeded without faculty input and oversight, which later emerged as a central critique of the process. There are a number of reasons why Chancellor Goldstein charged Dean Mogulescu with this project rather than inviting a group of seasoned faculty members to take the helm from the start. First, as is clear in the introduction to the concept paper, there were years of data to suggest that community college curricula and pedagogy were at least partly responsible for the substandard graduation rates. To rely on the same individuals who were viewed to have perpetuated the problem rather than addressing it seemed antithetical to the goals of the new community college project. Second, creating a new college with a radically altered mission and vision required system-level support and oversight. Traditional governing bodies, specifically the University Faculty Senate, were the incorrect spaces for which a new institution should be conceived. Their missions were too narrow in scope and unable to effectively bridge the operational, academic, and fiscal divides necessary to advance such a large-scale project. Lastly, Chancellor Goldstein had, in his time as chief executive of the university, consolidated a substantial amount of power and authority in the central office. Under his leadership, campus presidents reported directly to the chancellor rather than to the board of trustees and were held to a range of student outcomes and budgetary metrics on which their salary increases were determined. The new community college project was one in a series of examples of the central office demonstrating authority over the university, signaling to the campuses that organizational change that impacted the entire system could and would emerge from the chancellery.

This approach, however, narrowed the range of perspectives that went into conceptualizing the new community college. The base of research that informed the concept paper was organized around ideas that stemmed from several key individuals. This scholarship was and continues to be incredibly valuable to the community college sector, but the importance placed on this work by the planning team ignored a critical component of institutional development: *context*. The work of Dr. Thomas Bailey of the CCRC, for instance, spoke to the flaws in the community college sector nationally, underscoring the need for reform in remedial courses, advising, and degree pathways. Bailey and his colleagues presented substantive evidence that illustrated deleterious effects on student progress for those who were placed directly into zero-credit remedial courses.[25] Bailey is clear that, for most students, especially those who test close to the proficiency cut scores, time and money spent in remediation is unnecessary and slows academic momentum. He writes that, for these students, supplementary instruction in the way of peer tutoring often provides the requisite additional support.[26] Determining how best to integrate developmental skills with credit-bearing coursework, as Bailey suggests, requires a deep understanding of institutional context and culture. Drawing from Bailey's work, and other similar streams of research, the planning team determined that the best way to remediate students was through an integrative model that bridged credit-bearing work and developmental skills. They did so by increasing the number of contact hours of the first-year courses. Years of zero-credit remediation signaled that the stigma of being labeled "developmental" resulted in underperformance.[27] In an effort to move away from the policy of tracking students into zero-credit courses, however, the planning team reconfigured the remedial structure for the new college, ascribing all entering students with a remedial identity and requiring they enroll in scores of additional contact hours to become proficient. A critical assessment of institutional context may have discovered this problematic reconfiguration. However, the composition of the planning team did not include community college faculty or a diverse set of experts who deeply understood the institutional culture of remediation within the CUNY community colleges.

In addition to the limited range of research used in writing the concept paper, the planning team, at many points, overemphasized the possibility of working outside CUNY's traditional governance and administrative structures. Even as it faced a host of critical voices, including David Crook, university dean for institutional research and assessment, urging the planning team to frame its ambitious reforms within the realities of the university context, it failed to incorporate these recommendations into the final draft. Instead, Dean Mogulescu remarked that alterations to the concept paper would no doubt need to be made as the college prepared to open several years later. This lack of consideration for institutional context was apparent in several areas of the concept paper. One example that is, perhaps, most noteworthy, is the mechanism for awarding credit through the various stages of the first-year core. The planning team decided that faculty would award credit to students individually through ongoing portfolio-based assessment. Crook and others quickly noted that this approach would complicate matters such as financial aid awards that were contingent upon a student's completion of traditional Carnegie credit units. Another example, that will be discussed in detail in the next chapter, was workload expectations of faculty. The concept paper stated that faculty were expected to be in regular communication with students in class and electronically outside of regular classroom hours. Additionally, the concept paper called for faculty participation in summer bridge programs and institutional assessment work. CUNY, like many other university systems, is heavily reliant on a faculty union to determine the rigid workload structures within which faculty are employed and evaluated. Although operating outside of the traditional university bureaucracy appeared to be an ambitious move, it ultimately limited the new college's ability to conform to the standards of institutional governance.

Issues of Race

One of the most significant omissions from the concept paper and the planning process was a critical discussion of race as a central sociocultural factor of community college life at CUNY. Since remediation was abolished at the four-year colleges in 2000, the CUNY community colleges were the primary entry points for low-income students, students of color, first-generation and nontraditional students. As admissions standards to the four-year colleges continued to rise after 2000 and the demand for a college education increased, community college enrollment swelled. The concept paper rightly recognized that low completion rates were one indication that the community college sector was serving as a source of access but not of opportunity. In one way, the planning team designed a host of relevant student services that were proven to enhance student success. The positive early outcomes of the ASAP program provided a local lens through which similar services were constructed for the new college. On the other hand, the curriculum was organized around a deficit mindset that viewed students as highly underprepared, disadvantaged, and incapable of achieving at the college level without a substantial increase in time on task.

Culturally relevant curricula and pedagogy promote a caring and rigorous academic experience for those who have been marginalized by institutional racism. Gay writes that students who "are viewed negatively or skeptically are disadvantaged, often to the extent of total exclusion from participation in substantive academic interactions."[28] Although the concept paper was written five years before the new college enrolled its first class of students, the ways in which students were referenced in the paper set the tone for the culture of the college. In her discussion of culturally relevant teaching methodologies, Gay notes that "teacher expectations about students are affected by factors that have no basis in fact and may persist even in the face of contrary evidence."[29] The racial dynamics that would ultimately come to define the new institution emerged from generalizations about students in the community college sector. As a result, three central cultural tropes formed around the new college. First, *the wholesale application of remediation signaled to faculty, staff, and students that those who enrolled at the college were incapable of college-level work.* This, perhaps above all others, shaped the ways in which students have been understood and discussed. Since the curriculum was generated from this core belief, it served to reproduce inequities rather than challenge them. Second, *the expectation of increased time on task in the first-year core signaled to faculty, staff, and students that **all** of those who enrolled at the college were underprepared for college-level work.* This assumption failed to account for the diversity of ability in the student body and aligned the entire population with an expectation of deficiency. Third, *the planning team privileged skills-driven curricula over academic content.* This decision inevitably created barriers for students who were preparing to transfer to more traditional four-year institutions where discipline-specific content knowledge would be an expectation.

The absence of critical race theory and practice as essential components of the concept paper inadvertently created a culture of low expectations well before the college opened. The explicit ways in which students were referenced reproduced stereotypes instead of challenging them. For an institution that was poised to serve a large population of students of color, this misstep was consequential. In the case of the new community college, the voices that were privileged in its design played a significant role in how the college's culture formed. The absence of critical race theory and culturally responsive pedagogy meant that the college was organized without any substantive of the kinds of curricula and pedagogy that would best serve this population of students. Instead, the largely White planning team and advisory board predisposed the college to a culture of low expectations and deficit.

Looking Forward

The *New Community College Concept Paper* outlined an ambitious plan for CUNY's first new community college in over four decades. The concept paper drew from national research on best practices in associate's degree program reform. The educational model called for a radical revision to the traditional experience, detailing an innovative design for college-wide learning communities, intrusive advising, financial supports, and constructivist pedagogy. It placed itself in stark opposition to what had become the norm in remedial, vocational, and transfer-prep education. However, the concept paper was largely constructed in an isolated space within the university administration, led by Senior University Dean John Mogulescu and Director of Collaborative Programs Tracy Meade. Although the scope of reform was broad, the diversity of perspectives that guided the planning process was remarkably limited. This resulted in a number of critical oversights. For example, the issue of providing wholesale remediation was grounded in assumptions of ability based on race and racial bias. A more nuanced perspective, voiced by individuals more closely associated with community college students and their backgrounds, would have challenged the faulty assumption that all students would be at-risk and require remediation. This feedback, however, did emerge after the concept paper was distributed to a wider audience, but there is no indication that such cautionary commentary was taken into account. Rather, challenging academic content was abandoned in favor of a skills-driven, workforce-readiness academic culture that would eventually present a host of challenges for the institution and for its students who were preparing for transfer. The next chapter will discuss the shift from concept to college, beginning with the subsequent phases of the planning stage and the first year of the college's operation.

Notes

1. CUNY Newswire, "Reinventing Community Colleges," *News Release*, October 23, 2009.
2. City University of New York, *A New Community College Concept Paper* (New York, NY: City University of New York Office of Academic Affairs, 2008), 8.
3. City University of New York, 7.
4. City University of New York, 8.
5. City University of New York, 12.
6. City University of New York, 13.
7. City University of New York, 17.
8. City University of New York, 18.
9. City University of New York, 17.
10. City University of New York, 18.
11. City University of New York, 18.
12. City University of New York, 21.
13. City University of New York, 33.
14. City University of New York, 30.
15. City University of New York, 29.
16. City University of New York, 32.
17. City University of New York, 55.
18. Notes from meetings with community colleges to discuss concept paper for new community college, 2008.
19. Notes from meeting with community college caucus of University Faculty Senate, 2009, 4.
20. Notes from meeting, 4.
21. Letter from Regina Peruggi.
22. Letter from Gail Mellow.
23. Letter from Melissa Roderick.
24. Letter from David Crook.
25. Thomas Bailey, *Rethinking Developmental Education in Community College* (New York, NY: CCRC, 2009).
26. Bailey, 3.
27. Thomas Bailey, *Rethinking the Distinction Between Developmental and "College-Ready" Students in the Community College* (New York, NY: CCRC, 2008).
28. Geneva Gay, *Culturally Relevant Teaching: Theory, Research, and Practice* (New York, NY: Teachers College Press, 2018), 70.
29. Gay, 75.

2   From Concept to College

The Model

Phase two of the planning process began in January 2009. Dean Mogulescu and the planning team secured grants from the Bill & Melinda Gates Foundation, Carnegie Corporation, and the Josiah Macy Jr. Foundation, all of which supported the continued planning process. During the spring semester, a call went out to the university community for interested parties to participate in one of seven working groups. The first-round working committees were (1) City Seminar and Professional Studies, (2) Math Topics, (3) Assessment and Portfolios, (4) Enrollment and Persistence Management, (5) Library and Technology, (6) Facilities and Physical Infrastructure, and (7) FYE. A second round began shortly after and included (1) Center for College Effectiveness, (2) Governance and Organizational Structure, (3) Office of Partnerships, (4) Summer Bridge. Broadly, the committees were charged with devising critical pillars of the innovative educational model. Teams addressed questions regarding learning outcomes for the first-year core, how New York City would be used as a laboratory for student work, the modular structure in the first year, and criteria for awarding college credit.[1] Over the course of six months, committees authored reports detailing their proposals.

The FYE

Committees detailed an exhaustive admissions process that included multiple in-person individual and group interviews and plans for a robust Summer Bridge Program. At the time of the college's planning, Summer Bridge Programs were a postsecondary reform novelty. There had been some evidence to suggest that bridge programs, or extended orientations to college life, increase first-year retention and reduce summer melt, a term encompassing students who have applied and been accepted but fail to matriculate in the fall term. The new college's Summer Bridge Program was to begin at least two weeks ahead of the fall semester and provide students with an opportunity to build relationships with faculty and staff, be introduced to the first-year curriculum, nurture relationships with peers, and begin honing the kinds of collegiate habits required for sustained success. The committee recommended that the Summer Bridge curriculum be directly connected to the material in the FYE but that it be introduced in a low-stakes environment that promoted self-assurance and community building.[2] Conceptually, the Summer Bridge Program served as the gateway into the first year, onboarding both students and faculty in such a way that reduced the kinds of environmental shock endemic to a typical freshman experience.

The design of the FYE was significantly influenced by the framework laid out in the concept paper. Although the committee was responsible for developing the curricular structure for City Seminar and Professional Studies, members were mindful that the Math Topics course, discussed later, would be an integrated component of the first-year core. At the center of the design were a set of guiding principles that envisioned a series of courses that introduced students to disciplinary content in the social sciences, humanities, and sciences using an interdisciplinary lens and which also touched on skills development, including critical thinking, data analysis, and a range of higher-order skills.[3]

With New York City as a backdrop, City Seminar planned to address issues of public health, education, commerce, and environmental sustainability.[4] Through a series of problem-based modules across four linked sections, students would be introduced to a range of historical and sociological content that they could address as citizens of New York. The structure of City Seminar was essential for the integration of developmental skills and credit-bearing coursework. The case study component served as the hub for academic content and a space where students would be introduced to the historical and sociological concepts for the chosen public issue. The second component, an English class, supported the case study section by enhancing students' literacy and composition skills. A "Quantitative Reasoning" section acted as the third component of the City Seminar. In this section, students were introduced to data analysis skills relevant to the case study. Lastly, a Group Workspace component was imagined to serve as a supplementary instructional space where students would enhance basic skills, work on course material, and engage in group and individual advising sessions.[5]

Each 15-week semester included two seven-week modules with one week for faculty assessment and student advising. Over the course of the semester, the difficulty of student work was to increase as students moved from a deeply supportive educational model in the first term to a more independent approach in the second. Across all components, but especially in the "Quantitative" Reasoning section, faculty would choose data that was representative of the needs of a 21st century economy—including the growth of areas like the service and knowledge economies and the role of underrepresented groups in the workplace.[6] Among many design principles, the committee on City Seminar believed that students would benefit from a depth-over-breadth approach regarding the instruction of disciplinary content. Unlike the concept paper that focused heavily on issues of remediation, the plans for the first year as organized by the working group advanced a curriculum that viewed students as maturing learners, capable of handling complex material.[7] Unfortunately, this was never realized. Guttman's founding faculty developed a curriculum that presumed a low level of preparation and ability.

In conjunction with the City Seminar, the working group developed plans for another central component of the first year, Professional Studies. The economic situation during the planning period positioned community colleges as potential engines for job growth in highly skilled sectors. Plans for the new college emerged from a set of beliefs that rapid entry into the workplace from an associate's degree program was advisable. Although it became clear several years later that a broad swath of community college students desired bachelor's degrees, plans continued for designing the new college with a substantial focus on workforce readiness. Professional Studies was at the heart of this endeavor. The course planned to integrate a focus on major and career inquiry with the development of the kind of soft skills employers found attractive in new hires. Throughout the course, students would be presented with information related to various career pathways and the ways in which their educational trajectories might help them gain entry-level work. Additionally, Professional Studies was a place for students to engage with basic workplace competencies, including self-presentation, communication, and how to address critical feedback.[8] During instructional hours, students would work in teams to enhance skills in collaboration and workplace dialogue.

Along with drafting résumés, learning about internships, and discussing issues of salary negotiation, it was assumed that students in the Professional Studies course would have direct access to New York City employers. In cooperation with the proposed Office of Partnerships, faculty teaching the Professional Studies course linked their classes with employees from local businesses who would volunteer their time to come speak to students and offer on-site opportunities for students to explore the workplace.[9] The committee recommended that the college initially identify larger corporations with which to enter into partnership. This way, the maintenance of such partnerships would be logistically more feasible than attempting to coordinate with a greater number of smaller enterprises. From another standpoint, the committee noted, larger corporations could also serve as significant funding sources, as well as offering direct employment opportunities to students. Yet the economy changed rapidly during the early 2010s, propelling many college students toward a bachelor's degree. However, the Professional Studies course, later Ethnographies of Work, did not evolve alongside the labor market, leaving students exposed to material that was incongruent with their academic plans.

The last pillar of the FYE was a Math Topics course. The committee identified statistics as the required course for all students. This choice was made by evaluating the math requirements for the 12 proposed majors using examples from other CUNY colleges. Nine of the 12 majors listed in the concept paper required a course in statistics.[10] The committee also indicated that statistics courses prepare students for a broad range of professions and provide the quantitative skills necessary to enter into a highly skilled workforce. The proposed statistics course was to meet six hours per week and was modified to meet a range of educational backgrounds. As originally designed, the first semester statistics course would move at a slower pace, covering approximately half of an introductory-level course. At the end of the first semester, faculty assigned students to one of three math pathways based on their performance. The first, predicted to be the most common, was for students who successfully completed the first semester but required more time to complete the statistics course. They would continue their studies in the spring. Second, students who demonstrated competency and were ready to advance to more challenging work would complete their statistics material and move ahead into more complex algebra. This track was specially designed for students interested in STEM fields. Lastly, faculty would determine the best approach for students who were not successful in the statistics course in the first semester, including the possibility of a summer intensive.[11]

Full-Time Enrollment

Perhaps the most critical element to the Guttman Community College experiment was the requirement of full-time enrollment for all first-year students. There was a substantial amount of research that emerged during the recession era that pushed community colleges to encourage students to enroll full time.[12] There was evidence to suggest that students who enrolled full time in a community college were more likely to graduate than students who enrolled part time. Many factors contributed to increased momentum but paramount was a belief that students who felt they were part of the campus culture were more likely to persist than those who dropped in a couple of hours a week for a class. At CUNY, over two-thirds of community college students began as full-time matriculants but the percentage of those who remained full time after the first year steadily eroded as time went on. The traditional community college was not adequately set up to support full-time enrollment for students with busy lives. Required courses were often taught in opposing parts of the day, requiring students to trek back and forth to campus via public transportation or spend the gap in their day on campus with little or no activity. The reform movement in community college education sought to remedy this problem. At CUNY, the ASAP program was the first major initiative to offer students a block scheduling framework for their courses. Students who enrolled in the ASAP program were able to select from a series of courses that met back-to-back in either the morning or the afternoon. This condensed academic schedule created predictability from semester to semester and allowed students to better plan for their other obligations. This approach, however, required that students enroll full time.

The planning team incorporated the full-time requirement and block scheduling approach into the Guttman model. The mandatory full-time requirement is carefully explained to prospective students at the start of the lengthy admissions process. Although community colleges typically enroll a diverse student body which often includes a large percentage of nontraditional students, the requirement of full-time enrollment was a limiting factor for Guttman. Close to 100% of students have historically fallen between the ages of 18 and 23 and a majority enroll directly from a New York City public high school. The time-intensive model restricts those with family or work obligations from enrolling.

The concept of mandatory full-time enrollment in the community college sector is quite an anomaly. For decades, two-year institutions have prided themselves on enrolling a diverse subset of nontraditional students who otherwise found it impossible or undesirable to attend college full time. Yet with an abundance of research suggesting that full-time students are more likely to graduate on time coupled with a national policy agenda focused on increasing completion rates, Guttman positioned itself to attract students directly out of high school who were more likely to make the time commitment required of the model. By and large, CUNY community college students would rather be elsewhere. Years of survey data support claims that community college students, if given the opportunity, would much rather begin their college education at a four-year institution. Unlike in communities where two-year colleges serve the local population in workforce training, continuing education, and often act as the centers of civic culture, the community colleges at CUNY are, for many students, bridges that must be crossed on the way to something better.

Learning Communities and Block Scheduling

It is during Summer Bridge where students are first introduced to their learning community, or House, as it is called in the Guttman FYE. The concept paper did not imagine students would be assigned to traditional learning communities in the first year. Drawing on evidence of successful learning community implementation at Kingsborough Community College, the planning team recommended that students in the second- and third-year programs be organized into linked courses in a particular major. The practice of linking courses was common in learning communities. The modular structure of the FYE certainly would have allowed for relationship building among students in the various case study course sections, but the model also insinuated that as students mastered skills at different times during the academic year, they would be moved into new classes with other students of similar ability.

However, when the modular approach was abandoned prior to the college's opening, Guttman faculty transposed the learning community structure to the FYE and ultimately did not prepare for a similar structure in the programs of study. In so doing, the notion of what a learning community meant to the college deviated from traditional practice. When students arrived in the Summer Bridge Program, they were assigned to a House and a cohort. In the inaugural year, the college organized students into one of four Houses. In subsequent years, there has existed anywhere from five to seven Houses, given enrollment numbers in a particular year. Each House is composed of three cohorts, each with approximately 25 students. Teams of faculty are assigned to the House, each of whom serve as an instructor for one of the courses or course components of the FYE. Additionally, a student success advocate (SSA), or first-year advisor, is assigned to the House. The development of the House structure prior to opening in 2012 broadened the traditional definition of what a learning community meant to students and faculty. During Summer Bridge, students traveled through the various advising and curricular components with their cohort, with whom they remained in the majority of their courses in the FYE. Once they completed the Summer Bridge Program, students began the fall semester courses with their peers in their cohort.

The learning community model in the FYE evolved from the traditional paired course model to one where students in each cohort moved from course to course together throughout the first year at Guttman. In conjunction with this approach, the planning team also adopted a block scheduling framework, similar to what had been successfully implemented in the ASAP program, so that student schedules could be tightly controlled, and so working students would only have to attend class during a specified day part (morning or afternoon). Throughout the first years of the college's operations, students in the FYE have been expected to attend class every day. Each section meets for 90 minutes and spans five hours of each day. Initially, students were given an option at the time of enrollment to choose whether they would prefer to attend classes in the morning or the afternoon. Since 2016, entering students have been randomly assigned to one of three day parts (morning, afternoon, or evening). Students may appeal to the admissions office if there is a documented conflict that prevents them from attending during the assigned day part.

The unique learning community model Guttman adopted strictly controls the student experience. Although this arrangement allows for students to build relationships with their peers and with faculty in their House, it also has presented some challenges for many students. One student remarked that one of the biggest challenges of attending Guttman is the lack of flexibility, especially in City Seminar. The highly structured timetable does not include any breaks for students to work on projects or get individualized academic support. The learning community model, however, was designed to provide a universal experience for students regardless of their entering proficiency status. Randomly sorting students into cohorts ensured that the stigma of remediation and past academic performance were not considerations for placement at Guttman. The only form of tracking that was ultimately incorporated into the model was whether a student would enroll in one semester of statistics or take a stretched version that is spaced out in the curriculum over the course of a year.

Guided Pathways

The guided pathways model for community college education was created by Thomas Bailey and his team of researchers at the Columbia CCRC. It was designed in opposition to what Bailey referenced as the cafeteria model, or rather, the traditional community college structure which had historically mirrored that of the four-year colleges. Most importantly, the cafeteria model delivered unclear pathways toward completion for students. In the guided pathways framework, courses are clearly mapped to form tightly organized degree programs with limited choices and predictable schedules. The planning team relied heavily on the blueprint for a guided pathways college to conceptualize the academic and advising infrastructure for Guttman. At Guttman, students are introduced to the model in their various admissions interviews and first experience the schedule of classes in Summer Bridge. Given the proposed small size of the college initially, the planning team and founding faculty reduced the number of majors from 12 to 5. By only offering a handful of majors, there would be little opportunity for students to deviate too much in one direction or the other. Thomas Bailey wrote in a response to the Guttman model, "Given the amount of coordination and integration that you are proposing, the number that you propose seems like a lot. I realize that you are trying to provide more focused and defined majors or occupational programs within a college that still can be seen by students as a place to go before they choose their major. You have more or less set up a model in which students use one year to shore up their skills and decide which major or occupation they want and then they specialize in that area. This means that you have to have enough majors to offer students a relatively broad choice."[13] He argues that in order to establish efficient programs, the institution would have to support each major with enough faculty to plan, teach, and administer the educational enterprise. The small number of majors was a reasonable choice for both the faculty and students. By offering limited degree programs, the college could remain interdisciplinary and deliberately connect material learned by students in the FYE to the programs of study.

With this design, Guttman also satisfied another aim of the guided pathways framework. The model states that there should be "critical courses and other milestones" throughout the curriculum along with coherent and cohesive learning outcomes. On many community college campuses, students are free to take a range of classes as either degree requirements or electives in a given semester. Ultimately, it is assumed that each semester's courses will accumulate credits toward a degree. However, in so many cases, students accumulate credits but progress toward a degree is slowed because degree requirements are misunderstood, courses fill too quickly, majors are changed again and again, or a student takes a large number of electives. No matter the reason, time-to-degree is slowed. The Guttman academic model prescribes a series of courses in the first year that are taken in a strict sequence. During the fall 2 (winter) session, students who are meeting their FYE requirements may take a course that counts toward their major. This is the case, again, in the spring 2 (summer) session where more flexibility is available once the FYE courses are complete. Once all courses in the first year are successfully completed, students enroll directly into their program of study. Each of the five majors has a tightly sequenced set of courses with very few options for electives. In some cases, courses cross-list between majors so students have the opportunity to interact with individuals in other programs. In the final semester of a student's time at Guttman, he/she is required to take a capstone course that integrates texts, content, and skills from all the major courses into a culminating experience.

The guided pathways framework calls for instruction that is built from learning outcomes assessment. Shortly after its opening, Guttman faculty and administrators developed the Guttman Learning Outcomes (GLOs). The adoption of ePortfolios as the central repository for student work was in part a function of assessment. Once the GLOs were uniformly agreed upon by the faculty, GLO teams were organized to evaluate each learning outcome using artifacts from FYE and programs of study courses. A number of extensive reports have been issued that include detailed analyses of the GLOs. The GLOs underwent a period of revision. In 2018, the team charged with assessing the Broad Integrative Knowledge GLO presented its findings to the Guttman community. The learning outcome asks students to "integrate learning from broad fields of general study and connect different academic disciplines and multiple perspectives."[14] Faculty and staff on this committee determined that, within the discrete outcomes under the Broad Integrative Knowledge GLO, students made modest gains from Summer Bridge to the capstone course in their discipline. Similarly, a committee was charged with evaluating the Intellectual Skills GLO with a number of subcomponents. Findings from this group indicate that mathematical, research, and information literacy skills stall or reverse after students complete the FYE.[15] The findings from the GLO teams point to areas where curricular revisions can be made to enhance student learning. The outcomes assessment model, as recommended by the guided pathways approach, is serving the institution well as it strives to understand how best to nurture long-term student success.

Integrated Advisement

The concept paper detailed the importance of integrated student advising in the experimental model. Initially, it was believed that faculty teaching in the City Seminar would serve as student advisors. The planning team suggested that the bulk of student advising take place during the Group Workspace component of City Seminar where faculty could meet with students individually or in groups to ensure they were on track for success in areas like attendance, grades, due dates, and overall well-being.

After students completed the FYE, they were assigned an advisor in their major. Throughout the working committee's report writing period, it was anticipated that faculty would serve as student advisors. Between the time the concept paper was published and when the working committees finalized their reports, the only significant changes to the advising model were that faculty would partner with a student support specialist in Group Workspace to facilitate a wraparound student support program and that the curricular advising space would be connected with Ethnographies of Work. By the time the college opened, however, it had been determined that faculty would not serve as advisors. The college instead hired a team of SSAs for the FYE and career strategists for the programs of study who would serve as academic, career, and personal counselors for students.

SSAs supported student advisement in the FYE. To date, it has been the practice that there is one SSA assigned to each House in the fall and spring. The SSA typically holds one-on-one touchpoints with students throughout the academic year and is a member of the instructional team. In this role, the SSA attends weekly instructional team meetings, giving and receiving feedback on student performance, along with faculty. The SSA also serves as the central point of contact for student concerns, degree and financial planning, student social-emotional support, course registration, and myriad other issues. In the second year and beyond, students are assigned to career strategists who support their academic progress in the programs of study. Although there is not an instructional team model in the programs, the career strategists actively work to ensure they meet regularly with their assigned students, support faculty when student concerns arise, facilitate program-related activities, and prepare students for the transfer process.

The advisor's role at Guttman is unique in that the advising structure is an organizational component of the Office of Academic Affairs. In other institutions, advising services are housed separately. The planning team sought to remove the barriers between academics and advising by incorporating professional advisors into the academic enterprise. A recent evaluation of the ASAP program at Bronx Community College illustrates the critical importance of the advisor's role in long-term student success. Given the similar investment in student services and advising at Guttman, findings from a study of the impact of advising on student success would be comparable to the ASAP study. The downside to this model, however, is that it takes substantial buy-in in order to be effective. When there is a communication breakdown between groups, students often receive conflicting information or become the center of conflict between faculty and advisors.

Academic Technology

A hallmark of Guttman's innovative educational model is its commitment to the use of academic technology in the classroom and beyond. When the college opened in 2012, there was significant interest nationally on the effective use of ePortolios as pedagogical tools, allowing students to capture their work and reflect on previous assignments throughout their collegiate journey. Prior to opening, faculty and administration determined that all students would use ePortfolios in the classroom. The chosen platform, Digication, not only offered students the opportunity to upload their work to a unique portfolio and the ability to submit work electronically to instructors for grading, but it also permitted faculty and staff to conduct formative assessments directly within the system. Given the college's commitment to developing a culture of ongoing rigorous assessment, the utilization of ePortfolios as a central tool for such work minimized what is ordinarily a labor-intensive process.

Along with electronic portfolios, the college invested significant resources in outfitting classrooms with SmartBoard technology and laptops for each student. Additionally, the college made laptops available for student loan; acquired accessible devices, including scribe pens and headphones; and ordered classroom iPads. Along with these hardware acquisitions, Guttman has developed a rich software infrastructure through the Guttman portal. The college's Information Technology (IT) team, under the leadership of Chief Information Officer (CIO) John Stroud, has developed innovative and efficient mechanisms for the campus community to communicate with one another, request rooms, submit forms, and organize campus materials. In 2016, the college purchased a license with Starfish. Starfish operates as an early warning system, allowing faculty, advisors, and support staff to communicate with students regarding progress made in courses and necessary completion of administrative tasks, such as financial aid. Of its many qualities, Starfish is essential to student retention. Oftentimes, students at large community colleges are unable to determine how they are progressing in a course until the conclusion of the semester, making it difficult to recover. In many cases, this leads to high failure rates, particularly in gatekeeper courses, and ultimately high dropout rates. Guttman's commitment to providing the necessary supports needed to retain students means that faculty and advising staff are in constant communication with students regarding their progress and what modifications they need to make to be successful in their courses. Starfish offers the kinds of early alert notifications necessary to indicate to students throughout the semester where they stand in each course.

Peer Mentoring

When Guttman Community College opened, it quickly adopted a fully functional peer mentoring program led by Dr. Daniel Ambrose. What began with a small cadre of student mentors has expanded quite rapidly into a comprehensive service. Presently, students at Guttman who have completed their first year can apply to be one of our types of peer mentor. Admissions & Access peer mentors are often the first faces prospective students see when they come to Guttman. For students and families considering enrollment at the college, Admissions & Access peer mentors act as the main point of contact throughout the admissions process. Leading group and individual interviews, providing support at orientation, and leading sessions during Summer Bridge, these mentors are essential to shaping the early Guttman experience for incoming freshmen.

Throughout the FYE, students interact with FYE peer mentors. These mentors work directly with students who are enrolled in FYE courses. Each FYE peer mentor supports graduate coordinators in Studio and SSA's who facilitate the LABSS section of Ethnographies of Work. Throughout a student's first year at Guttman, FYE peer mentors support their development in a range of areas including effective study habits, time management, and general academic skills. Another group of mentors, meet-up peer mentors, also support the academic enterprise and enhance the student learning experience. During meet-ups, peer mentors engage with students who are seeking additional academic support in a particular subject area or class. These mentors have direct experience with the class for which they are leading the meet-up and assist students in weekly sessions as they work through major content areas or assignments. Lastly, transfer peer mentors engage with students at the conclusion of their Guttman journeys. For students are who are preparing to transfer to a four-year college, transfer peer mentors bridge the divide between Guttman and the receiving college. These mentors facilitate transfer workshops and provide critical support during the transition process. These students are graduates of Guttman and serve as key touchpoints on the four-year college campuses for Guttman students to connect with after transfer. This program is essential to the long-term academic health of Guttman graduates since the transfer process is often precarious and confusing for many community college students. Transfer peer mentors help to reduce transfer shock and ensure that graduates are retained beyond their first semester in the receiving institution.

The Center for College Effectiveness

At the center of the educational model was a commitment to ongoing institutional and learning outcomes assessment. Across committees, members agreed that shared rubrics and student ePortfolios would serve as the essential mechanisms for evaluating student work and thereby understanding the strengths and challenges of the educational model. In order to facilitate this work, the committee called for a Center for College Effectiveness (CCE) whose work would go well beyond that of a traditional office of institutional research. In order to effectively organize assessment processes and regularly disseminate findings, the CCE would establish a Center for Inquiry & Innovation whose efforts would bridge together institutional research and assessment and the responsibilities of a center for teaching and learning.[16] The committee laid out what it believed were the paramount reform practices central to the mission of the new college. They pointed to areas of student learning, such as the integrative developmental skills approach and mandatory full-time enrollment, and issues of alternative faculty roles and responsibilities that would be critical to assessment and evaluation.[17] Perhaps most importantly, the CCE was charged with serving as a neutral player in college operations, producing regular data-driven assessment reports for college stakeholders so that the experimental model could readily be adjusted based on findings. In this way, the CCE was imagined as a space free from typical intra-college politics, one that should not be seen as doing the work of the administration.[18] Its basic operations would include traditional institutional research in addition to acting as a space for faculty and administrative professional development and the main site at the college by which the major assumptions about student learning would be interrogated and revised.[19]

Under the leadership of a cabinet-level dean, the CCE was organized in such a way that it would retain central authority over facilitating institutional assessment but would, over time, identify other members of the college who would serve as scholars of practice in the center. The committee whose role was to conceptually design the CCE collaborated with the committee on assessment and ePortfolio to underscore the center's important role in driving assessment work across the college. In addition to this work, the committee recommended that the CCE create a college-wide database of student outcomes that could be easily accessed by faculty and staff.[20] In this way, data reporting could be linked to teaching practices and classroom assessment rubrics so that policy and pedagogy might be better aligned. Lastly, the committee believed the CCE could be a laboratory, serving as the central space within the college where revisions to the experimental model were articulated and from which new modes of instruction and operation emerged.

The working groups submitted their final drafts to the planning team in 2010. As the time drew nearer to the college's opening, the planning team began to search for a team of founding faculty. It was to be the responsibility of this core group of educators to operationalize what had been written both in the concept paper and in the work executed in committee.

Preparing to Open

On September 1, 2010, six founding faculty members met at an introductory dinner hosted by the planning team at the CUNY Graduate Center. The newly hired faculty, all junior and untenured, were initially appointed at other community college campuses in the CUNY system and given significant reassigned time to develop the curricular, governance, and bureaucratic systems for NCC at CUNY. By the time the founding faculty were hired, planning team staff had drawn up a blueprint for how faculty were expected to contribute to the development of Guttman Community College. At the center of the work was a commitment to substantially enhancing student success through a process of collaborative inquiry using evidence-based best practices.[21] There was significant emphasis placed on developing the FYE. Throughout 2010, faculty were scheduled to design the curriculum for City Seminar, Professional Studies, Math Topics, and the ways in which work in these courses would be assessed. Then, in 2011, the courses were to be piloted in CUNY's College Now, a program to help high school students earn college credits.

Faculty and Administrative Conflict

From the outset, and well into 2012, there was a great deal of discord between the faculty and the new administration. In January 2011, Dr. Scott E. Evenbeck was appointed as the Guttman's founding president. Prior to arriving in New York, Dr. Evenbeck was professor of psychology and dean of university college at Indiana University-Purdue University, Indianapolis. His experience in designing and leading first-year programs was attractive to CUNY senior leadership. A few months later, in August 2011, Guttman hired its founding provost, José Luis Morín, professor of Latin American studies at John Jay College and the college's interim dean of undergraduate studies. Neither individual had previous experience in either of the roles they now filled. Evenbeck, Morín, and the founding faculty were also operating against a backdrop of distrust that had emerged from the University Faculty Senate, the faculty union, and various national organizations. In 2010, the Professional Staff Congress, CUNY's faculty union, and the American Federation of Teachers (AFT) submitted a joint resolution, acknowledging issues of governance, academic rigor, resource management, and faculty workload in the plans for the Guttman. The resolution stated that the college's focus on accelerating the time to graduation came at the cost of academic quality and rigor. In addition to their concerns regarding the curriculum, the AFT/Professional Staff Congress (PSC) resolution recognized that the NCC was largely without a traditional governance structure and was reliant upon the planning team to lead. However, once Guttman had hired a president and provost, it was clear that standard faculty responsibilities, particularly with regard to the role of department chairs, were without definition.[22]

The founding faculty also encountered significant alterations to the educational model shortly after they were hired. Facing institutional restrictions on the kinds of experimentation the planning team had initially devised, including how credits were to be awarded, modifications were made to the FYE that curtailed preliminary expectations. For example, the modular approach to the academic year was abandoned, prompting faculty to work within a more traditional structure. Guttman instead adopted a 12-6 calendar: 12 weeks of a fall 1 term plus an additional 6 weeks of a fall 2 term, giving students who were not successful in their first term time to recuperate in the subsequent 6 weeks. Within this framework, the City Seminar curriculum retained its case study focus but transitioned to a 10.5-hour per week course with three components meeting 3 hours per week in addition to 1.5 hours of Group Workspace. The additional hours in the classroom provided an alternative to zero-credit remediation. By 2011, the faculty had reimagined Professional Studies as well. The course ultimately took the name Ethnographies of Work and included a more focused introduction to sociological concepts related to labor studies while maintaining an emphasis on career readiness. Lastly, Guttman settled on a course in statistics to satisfy the university's basic math requirement.

In order to begin working on the curriculum for each of the new first-year programs, the founding faculty proposed a preliminary college council so that curricular matters could be funneled through a governance structure.[23] President Evenbeck argued that the college was too small and not developed enough for a formal governance structure with a range of committees. On the one hand, his intuition was correct. Several years later when the college adopted a more robust governance plan, it was too cumbersome for its current operational resources. On the other hand, however, some members of the founding faculty asserted that attempts to stall the creation of a governance plan were efforts by the administration to retain control over the direction of the college.[24] As the protests of the faculty grew evermore public, the administration responded and organized several task forces, including one on governance. Discussions on how the governance structure of the new college should be organized, issues that will be covered in detail in the next chapter, were accented by key mandates which were supported by senior leadership in the CUNY central office. For example, the president and senior staff were committed to a college without academic departments, a principle that originated from Dean Mogulescu's office and one that the faculty resented from the outset. Many in the CUNY central administration believed that academic departments stalled institutional reform and protected worn curricula and tired pedagogies. At the system level, there was evidence to suggest this belief was firmly grounded in reality. Initiatives aimed at reconstructing the general education requirements, for example, had failed in the 1990s in large part because of department opposition. For the founding faculty at Guttman, the preliminary governance plan that was eventually adopted was organized without their input.

The political landscape at Guttman led to the departure of several founding faculty. One faculty member was asked to leave after stating his opposition to the lack of academic departments. After the plan was adopted in 2012, the debate around shared governance continued. One faculty member resigned that spring, and another quickly followed a week later citing "toxic institutional politics."[25] The views of some founding faculty members signaled that the administration, in particular Provost Morín, was responsible for creating a culture that silenced dissent and viewed opposition and disagreement as heretical.[26] At the same time, Guttman was decidedly a different college than most. It was designed by senior administration with little faculty input and had gained such national acclaim that the university believed it had to be tightly controlled in order for it to succeed. By the start of 2012, the political infighting at Guttman had delayed the development of the curriculum, leading to a rushed implementation process as plans proceeded to open in the fall.

The First Year

The Curriculum

On August 20, 2012, approximately 300 students and a team of faculty and staff met for the first time at the opening convocation for the NCC at CUNY. In the grand banquet hall of the historic New York Public Library on Fifth Avenue, the college welcomed its inaugural class. Much had changed for Guttman since the concept paper had been written five years prior. The educational model only somewhat resembled the design laid out in the concept paper and had evolved even further from the specifications recommended by the working committees in 2010.

The development of the learning community structure had evolved quite substantially during the planning process. In the months leading up to the college's opening, significant attention was paid to how students would be organized in the FYE. The inaugural class consisted of 289 students, organized into four Houses, or learning communities, each with three cohorts of approximately 25 students. In a significant departure from the plans in the concept paper, the college hired a team of four SSAs to serve as advisors to students in their first year. The SSAs became an integral component of the House structure, meeting weekly with faculty teaching the first-year courses to discuss student progress, pedagogy, and classroom management.

City Seminar emerged as the educational core of the learning community model. In the final phase of the planning process, the focus of the Group Workspace component of City Seminar became a political flashpoint. The initial plan was for Group Workspace to be led by a faculty member in the instructional team and the space for student advising. However, in negotiations about faculty workload, it was determined that Group Workspace did not qualify as a course but rather a supplemental instructional space for which faculty could receive workload credit. Some faculty believed that the college's administration decided to forego faculty instruction in Group Workspace to save money, employing graduate students or peer mentors as facilitators rather than apply workload credit to full-time professors.[27] This conflict resulted in a rocky start for Group Workspace. Graduate students, titled graduate coordinators, primarily from the CUNY Graduate Center were employed at the last minute to facilitate an ill-defined Group Workspace. Unlike the rest of the FYE, the curriculum for Group Workspace was vague and without a clear direction. For 90 minutes per week, students were intended to focus on skill-building in conjunction with the work that was being completed in City Seminar. However, it quickly became apparent that attempts to align the content and foci of City Seminar and the work that needed to be done in Group Workspace were complicated tasks. They required faculty to have several weeks of lessons drawn up in order for the graduate coordinator to effectively plan for the time in Group Workspace. In most cases, this was not possible and did not happen, and it left the graduate coordinator scrambling to create activities that were adjacent to the work in City Seminar.

For math faculty, there was trouble regarding how students would pass the CUNY-mandated algebra exam. The CUNY Elementary Algebra Final Exam (CEAFE) was a requirement for all undergraduates who did not enter college with earned algebra credits. Although NCC did not have zero-credit remedial classes, it did use the entering mathematics placement exam, COMPASS, to determine whether a student was placed into a one-semester statistics course or a stretched version, one in which the material was paced over an entire year. For students who had not demonstrated algebra proficiency at the time of entry and were placed in the stretched version of statistics, 35% of their course grade in the spring semester was determined by success on the CEAFE exam. Since the mathematics model at the NCC attempted to circumvent the traditional algebra requirement other colleges enforced, the university's requirement that students pass the CEAFE presented a challenge to the faculty. Much of the preparation for the math curriculum focused on concepts in statistics and the data analysis skills necessary for the quantitative reasoning component of City Seminar. However, there was little in the way of curricular preparation for the CEAFE exam, and faculty were not prepared to teach algebra in any of their courses. The makeshift approach for the first two years, until the university began accepting alternatives to the CEAFE in 2014, was for math faculty to dedicate part of their semester in statistics to teaching basic algebra concepts and spend time in quantitative reasoning doing the same. The imposition of CEAFE preparation in the quantitative reasoning curriculum meant that this component was, at times, out of step in terms of content with the rest of City Seminar.

Just as the college was opening, CUNY was ending a drawn out and very public battle with the faculty and the Professional Staff Congress over a proposed resolution to reconstruct the undergraduate general education requirements. The Pathways Initiative, spearheaded by then-executive vice chancellor and university provost Alexandra W. Logue, had rattled the bedrock of the university since 2011. Broadly, the proposal recommended a uniform set of general education requirements to ease transfer between the colleges and decrease the number of excess credits a student accumulated as a result of disparate requirements. Pathways was a victory for community college students, the majority of whom wanted a bachelor's degree. A vocal group of faculty members and the PSC joined forces to oppose it, charging the university with obfuscating shared governance policies and attempting to force a curriculum onto the colleges. The university won two court cases, and Pathways was implemented with little fanfare in 2013. Guttman, however, had to go back to the first-year curriculum and modify its introductory courses to align with the new Pathways disciplinary areas. Although the structure of courses like City Seminar did not change, there was substantial revision to the curriculum. City Seminar I, for example, had to be retrofitted to meet the standards for the World Cultures and Global Issues area of the Pathways

Common Core while City Seminar II was adjusted to satisfy the requirements for U.S. experience in its diversity. Although the necessary Pathways adjustments were subtle and did not necessitate substantial revisions to the Guttman model, these changes did force the new college to consider how its curriculum was part of the larger university landscape, a task that challenged its origin story of uniqueness.

Leadership and Staffing

In preparation for the opening day of Summer Bridge, the founding faculty and administration went about hiring new faculty, advisors, and key staff members. Since there were no departments or chairs and a small administrative team, several inaugural faculty members (second wave of hires) were onboarded with hybrid-administrative roles. For example, the college hired Laura Gambino, previously a professor at Tunxis Community College who had experience with learning outcomes assessment as a professor of information technology with expertise in ePortfolio and assessment. Under this arrangement, Gambino was hired to partner with the CCE to develop the college's institutional learning outcomes and assessment plan. She was also responsible for operationalizing the ePortfolio program at scale, providing students and faculty with training on how to use portfolio-based learning in the classroom. Another similar hire was Dr. Ariana Gonzalez-Stokas who was hired as a professor of interdisciplinary studies with expertise in peer mentoring. Along with her teaching responsibilities Gonzalez-Stokas was charged with building a robust mentoring model that was intended to provide instructional and co-curricular support. Other members of the faculty held hybrid roles as well. English professor Claire King was responsible for organizing the college's experiential education program, specifically community days, dedicated time in the calendar for students to volunteer and participate in service-learning projects.

The role of instructional team leader was critical in the first year of the college's operation. One faculty member from each of the four Houses was chosen by the provost to serve as its team leader. This individual was responsible for organizing weekly instructional team meetings, organizing House functions, and serving as a liaison to the provost. Although this was a crucial leadership role within the House structure, the position of instructional team leader did not carry the same weight or responsibility of a department chair at a traditional college. These individuals did not have supervisory authority over the faculty teaching in the House nor were they able to make decisions regarding scheduling, curriculum, or weigh in on personnel matters. However, faculty teaching in the FYE valued the instructional team leader and looked to this individual as a necessary buffer between them and the administration.

The planning team, and eventually the administration, made every effort to organize the educational model in such a way that the majority of classes were staffed by full-time faculty. On the other community college campuses at CUNY, the percentage of adjunct faculty exceeded the number of tenure-track professors. However, to fill staffing gaps, several adjunct faculty members were hired at the start of the first Summer Bridge Program. These individuals were given a full workload of three courses and were integral members of the instructional team. Unlike traditional colleges where adjuncts typically did not participate in the daily operations of the institution, Guttman fully integrated the part-time faculty members. Adjuncts were routinely included in college governance meetings, invited to facilitate professional development workshops, and asked to serve on various committees.

A number of faculty from other CUNY institutions served as senior advisors in the role of consortial faculty. These individuals who advised relatively junior NCC faculty in key areas like English composition and basic math provided some of the leadership that senior faculty would typically offer in a traditional institution. Kim Sanabria, professor of English at Hostos Community College, led a number of professional development workshops for writing faculty and helped to design the reading and writing curriculum for City Seminar. Estela Rojas at New York City College of Technology offered guidance for faculty in basic mathematics. In addition to the consortial faculty, a number of retired administrators served as counselors to the provost and president on operational matters. Larry Mucciolo, former CUNY deputy chancellor, developed logistical plans for how best to increase the college's enrollment and scale-up the educational enterprise. Stephanie Benjamin, former associate dean for academic affairs at CUNY, spearheaded Guttman's faculty search processes. These individuals played critical roles during the college's start-up phase and were slowly replaced by permanent staff.

Lessons for Higher Education

Organizational Development

The early conflicts between the faculty and administration were due, in large part, to the lack of compatibility between the concept and operational realities of the NCC. There were key mistakes made early on that contributed to the dissolution of institutional unity just before the college opened. The NCC initiative did not employ senior, tenured founding faculty members. There are several possible reasons why the decision was made to hire inexperienced, untenured assistant professors to take command of the educational enterprise for the new college. One such reason dates back to how the planning team was first organized, a topic discussed in detail in the preceding chapter. Since the members of the planning team, and eventually the working committees, were drawn largely from areas outside the mainstream academic enterprise at CUNY, there was insufficient consideration for how best to create a robust and knowledgeable faculty and administration. Inexperienced senior administrators were paired with junior faculty in an organizational setting that was not yet defined. Traditionally, tenured faculty provide a layer of advocacy between junior faculty and the administration. These individuals often act as department chairs, which Guttman did not have, and as advisors to their junior colleagues throughout the precarious tenure process. Without the guidance and leadership of senior faculty, the newly appointed Guttman faculty members fell prey to the normal anxieties of pre-tenure employment that were compounded by the absence of structure and concrete responsibilities, along with the added pressure of executing a lofty mission.

Although tenured founding faculty members would not have fully alleviated the organizational strife in the lead-up to the college's opening, seasoned faculty would have. If strategic hiring decisions had been made, such appointments would have afforded the faculty a disciplined and steadied voice in crafting institutional policy. Many of the setbacks in the final stages of planning, especially with regard to the curriculum, were a result of the discord between the faculty and the administration. These conflicts occurred because inexperienced faculty and administrators were operating without precedent and institutional history. Absent the conviction of experience and the stability that comes with tenure, the founding faculty scrambled to protect their jobs and advance the vision of the college in a highly pressurized environment. In turn, the provost and president viewed faculty opposition as insubordinate and antagonistic. These conflicts were symptomatic of inexperience in critical areas of the new college's operations.

Adjusting Expectations

This disjuncture between the planning team and traditional academic protocol at CUNY meant that significant adjustments had to be made to the educational model in the latter stages of the planning process. The revolutionary design laid out in the concept paper had to be tempered in order to adjust to system-level operational standards. This process was largely left to the inexperienced founding faculty. As a result, blind spots emerged in the model that stymied the institution's maturation. First, there was insufficient development of the embedded developmental skills model, including how basic skills would be taught alongside college-level content and what sorts of professional development new faculty would need to ensure that this critical component was being addressed. When the college opened, faculty were introduced to skills spines for City Seminar, a series of documents indicating what basic skills were to be covered at each stage of the semester, but there was little in the way of preparation for how these skills would be addressed pedagogically. Rather than focusing on specific basic skills, the additional time on task in City Seminar became the rationale for how Guttman addressed remediation. However, it became consistently unclear how these additional hours were supporting basic skills development and for what they were being used. Second, when the planning team recognized that university policy would not allow for faculty to award course credit in a piecemeal fashion, plans were not made for how students would move through the first year if they were unsuccessful in a course. There was an initial proposal suggesting that the six-week sessions be used for recuperation. Students who were unsuccessful in the 12-week session would earn a grade of No Credit (NC) so that their GPA would not be negatively impacted, and they would spend the subsequent 6-week session completing substandard or outstanding work. However, a six-week session of City Seminar was never created. Consequently, students who did not earn a passing grade in the 12-week semester were required to retake the full 10.5-hour-per-week course again in the following 12-week semester, significantly slowing their time-to-degree.

There are other examples of blind spots that resulted from how faculty and administrators adjusted the educational model in the year leading up to the college's opening. Many of these adjustments, however, were the product of inappropriate planning. As was discussed in the preceding chapter, the one-size-fits-all model of remediation presented a host of problems. It was inconceivable that this approach would, in the long run, adequately serve all students. Without proper attention to the basic skills component, those students who would have benefited from additional classroom time focused on developmental education did not receive the necessary instruction. Conversely, the additional time on task was unnecessary for students who arrived at Guttman ready to do college-level work. It also should have been clear that the approach to the awarding of credit was not reasonable within a public university system responsible to state and external accrediting bodies. The radical vision of the concept paper and many of the recommendations that emerged from the working committees were both bold and unrealistic. Many of the issues that the college faced in its first decade ensued from misaligned ambition. Since the planning team worked almost entirely outside the traditional academic infrastructure, their intentions did not match well with the realities that eventually faced the founding faculty and administration. A more focused approach to innovation would have set Guttman on more solid ground in its first years. It would be the responsibility of the subsequent provosts, deans, and faculty members to more effectively position the college within the framework of university policy and practice.

Notes

1. The New Community College Initiative, *The New Community College First Round Working Committee Reports* (New York, NY: The New Community College Initiative, March 2010), 8.
2. The New Community College Initiative, *The New CUNY Community College Second Round Working Committee Reports* (New York, NY: The New Community College Initiative, September 2010), 102.
3. The New Community College Initiative, *The New Community College First Round Working Committee Reports* (New York, NY: The New Community College Initiative, March 2010), 9.
4. The New Community College Initiative, 12.
5. The New Community College Initiative, 13.
6. The New Community College Initiative, 15.
7. The New Community College Initiative, 22.
8. The New Community College Initiative, 24.
9. The New Community College Initiative, 29.
10. The New Community College Initiative, 42.
11. The New Community College Initiative, 45–46.
12. Thomas Bailey, Shanna Smith Jaggars, and Davis Jenkins, *Redesigning America's Community Colleges: A Clearer Path to Student Success* (Cambridge, MA: Harvard University Press, 2015).
13. Thomas Bailey, Comments on *"A New Community College Concept Paper."*
14. Broad Integrative Knowledge GLO Assessment Report (2018).
15. Intellectual Skills GLO Assessment Report (2017).
16. The New Community College Initiative, *The New CUNY Community College Second Round Working Committee Reports* (New York, NY: The New Community College Initiative, September 2010), 11.
17. The New Community College Initiative, 12–13.
18. The New Community College Initiative, 14.
19. The New Community College Initiative, 14.
20. The New Community College Initiative, 19.
21. Memorandum, *The New Community College Initiative on Faculty Development in the New Community College* (New York, NY: Memorandum, September 2010).
22. American Federation of Teachers & Professional Staff Congress of CUNY, *Implications of a New Model for Community Colleges: The City University of New York* (New York, NY: American Federation of Teachers & Professional Staff Congress of CUNY, 2010).

23. Bill Rosenthal and Emily Schnee, "The New Community College at CUNY and the Common Good," *Thought and Action* 29 (Fall 2013): 91.
24. Rosenthal and Schnee, 92.
25. Rosenthal and Schnee, 94.
26. Rosenthal and Schnee, 96.
27. Rosenthal and Schnee, 96.

3 Issues of Administration and Governance

In April 2013, NCC at CUNY officially became Stella and Charles Guttman Community College. The Guttman Foundation awarded the college a $15 million endowment, the largest gift ever awarded to a CUNY college. As the college began to establish its newly formed identity within the CUNY system, it was clear that years of complicated work lie ahead to create the robust infrastructure necessary to manage a complex college. Early conflicts between the faculty and administration signaled that the absence of a cohesive governance structure and ill-defined job responsibilities were poised to cause continued disruption on campus. This chapter will discuss challenges that faced key administrative positions as the college grappled with its management structure. This will then move into a discussion of how Guttman organized its first operational governance plan.

Administration

The President

Dr. Scott E. Evenbeck was appointed Guttman's founding president in 2011 before there was a building or students. President Evenbeck arrived in New York City from his position as dean at Indiana University-Purdue University, Indianapolis. Chancellor Goldstein chose Evenbeck for the job because of his experience building first-year programs. A psychologist by trade, President Evenbeck enthusiastically supported the tenets of the Guttman model. The role of founding president in a highly visible and controversial college came with myriad challenges. Evenbeck was thrust into controversies with the faculty, the union, and CUNY's central office in the days ahead of the college's opening. There was a substantial amount of pressure on the college's first president to realize the multidimensional educational model and to ensure that the institution effectively achieved its completion benchmarks. For Evenbeck, these many responsibilities required him to delicately navigate the complex CUNY political sphere.

Guttman's founding president was in a delicate and highly visible position from the outset. Since the institution had set itself apart from the traditional community college model, its ability to reach its anticipated outcomes was highly scrutinized. Not only was President Evenbeck responsible for achieving graduation and retention metrics, but he was also charged with maintaining the operational model. The founding faculty were resistant to what they believed was a top-down administrative structure and advocated for traditional governing bodies and departmental representation in the two years before the college opened. However, Guttman's identity was organized around being different, and President Evenbeck was responsible for promoting the college as a unique alternative to the tired community college experience. President Evenbeck drew a line in the sand for the faculty. He feared that any alteration to the model, educational and administrative, would erode Guttman's public appeal. Initially, the faculty demanded a traditional governance model and wanted to organize themselves into departments. President Evenbeck, however, resisted this approach and directly communicated to the faculty that Guttman would never have academic departments while he was president. The faculty viewed this as a usurpation of their professional rights but Evenbeck, rather, believed any such organization would jeopardize the college's ability to retain an interdisciplinary and nimble curricular structure. The issue of governance and departmental organization was multifaceted. On one hand, Evenbeck recognized that a departmental structure in such a small institution would create the exact divisions and silos that Guttman was designed to eradicate. On the other hand, the belief that departments would stymie necessary curricular revision was erroneous. In fact, the absence of academic leadership and the flattened organizational structure stalled the kind of responsiveness the planning team had in mind for the college.

The lack of traditional academic leadership roles also meant that President Evenbeck played a more active part in personnel decisions than a typical college president. For Evenbeck, it was imperative that the public portrayal of the college be positive. Under the CUNY collective bargaining agreement and the local reappointment, promotion, and tenure process, faculty are, by and large, awarded professional milestones by their peers. The president of the college has the authority to overturn decisions made by the college personnel committee without justification. Throughout President Evenbeck's tenure at Guttman, he made several controversial personnel decisions that contradicted the recommendation set forth by the personnel committee. In almost all cases where President Evenbeck intervened, it was because the personnel committee had made a negative decision regarding a faculty member that he believed should be overturned. There were several examples of this early in the college's history. Unsurprisingly, faith in the peer review process was tarnished. In an effort to avoid conflict and to keep the college in a positive light with members of the central administration, President Evenbeck used his authority in the personnel process to disrupt potential negative actions on the part of affected faculty. The reversal of negative personnel actions furthered the belief that the faculty had no input in traditional academic matters and that efforts at shared governance were a façade.

The excitement around the Guttman brand was short-lived. During the planning phase and throughout the first two years of operation, faculty and staff from Guttman presented widely on the efficacy of the model, highlighting the high retention and graduation rates of the inaugural class as evidence of success. Colleges from the United States and around the world visited Guttman, and President Evenbeck rolled out the red carpet for numerous leaders who hoped to copy some of what Guttman had instituted. After a few years, though, interest in the college faded. Much of what was unique about Guttman during the planning phase became ubiquitous. The recession era prompted community college leaders to invest in advising, guided pathways, and in the scholarship of teaching and learning. The three-year completion rate declined by almost ten percentage points, hovering around 40% for the 2016 entering class. Transfer data that showed Guttman students flagging in comparison to their CUNY peers became public and the cost of the model became difficult to justify. President Evenbeck was faced with a difficult decision. The remedy to the low educational outcomes meant recognizing that the Guttman model was, in large part, ineffective. The pieces of the model that were most impactful and influential, advising and mandatory fulltime enrollment, were overshadowed by the failures of the curriculum. Yet it was the curriculum that perceivably set Guttman apart from the other community colleges. If President Evenbeck supported a wholesale reorganization of the academic experience, it would be to admit Guttman's failure. To press on meant that many more students would suffer but that the charade of innovation and experimentation could be kept up, even if just for a little longer.

For most of his tenure, President Evenbeck was caught between Guttman's mythology and its reality. There was an intense desire among faculty and administration to maintain Guttman's image as a diamond in the rough, a college that had truly risen above the systems and policies that had plagued other institutions. The reality, though, was far more complex. There were elements of the Guttman model that were excellent investments. Charles Pryor, Daniel Ambrose, and Bindi Patel led a team of committed advisors who helped students persevere and succeed. But the emphasis on the curriculum and its prominence in how Guttman was portrayed to an external audience prevented critical change from happening. Wholesale change to the model would come after President Evenbeck retired in July 2020.

The Provost

Provost José Luis Morín arrived at Guttman shortly after President Evenbeck. As a former lawyer and academic, Morín was logistically minded, formal, and committed to executing the Guttman model. The provost's office faced a number of challenges early on. Morín quickly established himself as head of the faculty. In ordinary custom, the chief academic officer of a collegiate institution would, in title, be responsible for the faculty. However, daily operational oversight would be distributed among a host of deans, department chairs, and program coordinators. When Guttman opened in 2012, there was no hierarchical buffer between the faculty and provost. Provost Morín held visible positions on the Curriculum Committee, the college's personnel committee, college council, and on other ad hoc task forces. The provost also presided over faculty meetings and organized faculty teaching schedules, observations, and annual reviews. Morín's office quickly became overburdened with operational tasks, which prevented him from setting the academic direction of the college. One of the most significant obstacles Morín faced in this regard was the college's lack of preparation to execute the programs of study in the 2013–2014 academic year. Morín, as well as the faculty, spent the latter part of the planning phase developing the FYE. Although the six programs of study were established at the time of opening, there had been only limited curricular development. Also, with only 18 full-time faculty, it was unclear how the programs were to be staffed in comparison to the labor-intensive first year. These pressures added to the managerial difficulties in the provost's office. Morín submitted his resignation effective January 2014. Provost's Morín's experience as Guttman's first provost set the stage for the challenges each of his successors would face as the college slowly built an administrative apparatus necessary to support the chief academic officer.

Joan M. Lucariello was appointed interim provost of Guttman Community College in February 2014. Provost Lucariello was a former psychology professor and senior administrator in CUNY's central office. She brought to Guttman a wealth of experience in university management and a pragmatic spirit aimed at helping the college to streamline its programs in preparation for a period of growth. Lucariello was a researcher by trade and asked questions regarding the institution's financial health, the effectiveness of each of its programs, and how the college should organize itself bureaucratically in order to be more efficient. These questions involved interrogating the effectiveness of the Guttman model, using data to understand trends in student and program outcomes. At this point in the college's history, there was a culture that directly opposed criticism of the educational model. President Evenbeck's insistence that the Guttman narrative be consistently positive was mirrored by members of the faculty and staff. Challenges to the status quo were harshly quieted. Provost Lucariello also sought to create an additional layer of bureaucratic hierarchy in the Office of Academic Affairs. Although José Morín appointed a dean of academic affairs, this appointment was only briefly filled and supplied only superficial relief to the provost's office. Lucariello, instead, hired three associate deans to absorb many of the operational responsibilities ineffectively held by the provost's office. Laura M. Gambino was promoted from the faculty to serve as associate dean for assessment and technology, Patricia Price was hired to oversee research and the programs of study, and Marissa Schlesinger was brought in from Kingsborough Community College to lead the FYE, scheduling, and the learning communities. President Evenbeck, however, hesitated to grant Lucariello the supervisory authority over the three deans, as is typical of a traditional college. Evenbeck, firmly committed to a flattened hierarchical structure, saw Lucariello's reconstruction of the Office of Academic Affairs as antithetical to the tenets of the college. Recognizing Lucariello's compromised position, each of the three deans operated independently of one another, leading their own initiatives with little discussion and coordination as a unit. Lacking support from her deans and the college's president, Lucariello was dismissed by President Evenbeck in early 2017.

Former Kingsborough Community College provost Stuart Suss was appointed as Guttman's interim provost in June 2017. Provost Suss maintained the Office of Academic Affairs for just under a year until April 2017 when Howard Wach was hired as the college's next permanent provost. Under Wach's leadership, the college's administrative apparatus has been largely stabilized, and the academic enterprise is engaged in critical assessment activities to understand how the model can best be scaled to serve more students. Provost Wach has appointed three new academic deans, each of whom oversees critical areas of academic affairs. Lavita McMath Turner serves as assistant dean of equity, inclusion, and experiential learning; Nicola Blake serves as dean of faculty affairs; and Niesha Ziehmke as associate dean of programs and planning. Unlike his predecessors, Wach has maintained an active working relationship with President Evenbeck. This working relationship has afforded the Office of Academic Affairs an opportunity to launch a range of initiatives aimed at strengthening the Guttman model. Wach has spearheaded college-wide programs related to equity, diversity, and inclusion. During his tenure, advances in university-wide technology gave the CUNY colleges tools to examine real-time data related to student outcomes. Provost Wach immediately sought to address inequities in student performance. One of the most striking revelations, a topic that will be discussed fully in a later chapter, was the lackluster performance of Guttman students who transferred to a CUNY four-year college after graduation. To address these issues, Wach partnered with CUNY community colleges, the Bronx College and Lehman College, forming the Bronx Transfer Affinity Group (BTAG), a grassroots collaborative designed to create nurturing and efficient pathways for transfer students between the campuses. The poor transfer outcomes, however, were symptomatic of larger cultural issues at Guttman. In the years since Guttman opened, CUNY made significant alterations to the guidelines around remediation and basic skills proficiency. Evidence from independent studies showed promising results in corequisite courses in mathematics in comparison to years of troubling outcomes in zero-credit courses. As the slow shift to adopt more equitable developmental skills curricula gained traction at CUNY, Wach was forced to reconcile why Guttman continued to require so many hours of remediation for all of its students.

Provost Wach's tenure was defined by challenging and critical discussions of race relations at Guttman. Necessary shifts to the curriculum were shaped by dialogue about the institution's history and the cultural assumptions about race, ability, and expectations that shaped the college's early culture. Wach charged Dean Lavita McMath Turner with leading broad and complicated conversations about equity and diversity. With strong advocacy and community organizing experience, McMath Turner recruited external practitioners, organized professional development on culturally responsive pedagogy, and engaged with faculty and staff in formal and informal settings to discuss the harmful effects of racism and to plan a better way forward for the college. Provost Wach has consistently supported this work and continues to navigate the college as it takes action to correct its past.

It was during Provost Wach's time at Guttman that the curricular work necessary to address the inequities evidenced in the educational model began. One of Wach's major initiatives was the revision of City Seminar, a project that spanned most of his first three years and one that would come to define his relationship with the faculty. Deans McMath Turner and Blake were primarily responsible for the revision. Under their leadership, a team of faculty worked for over two years to put together a more equitable proposal for the course. It was during this time that Wach came into direct conflict with the views of the faculty. His senior academic administrative team recognized that the structure of the course had to change in order to effectively support students, but they also acknowledged that the FYE was neither fiscally sustainable nor scalable in its current format. The faculty members leading the revision effort, however, were, at least in part, resistant to abandoning the original model because it afforded them a desirable teaching schedule that was supported by a reduced teaching load for serving on an instructional team. Plans to reduce the contact hours of the course threatened this arrangement. Provost Wach also challenged expensive programs like Global Guttman, the study abroad initiative that sent faculty and students around the world, that was fully supported by college funds. Although Provost Wach was a cautious administrator, he was very much supported in this effort to alter City Seminar by members of the senior academic administration. Ultimately, a compromise was reached during the 2020–2021 academic year.

Governance

Personnel Matters

During Provost Stuart Suss's tenure, the college organized a governance task force to draft the framework for Guttman's first comprehensive shared governance plan. Until 2016, Guttman operated from the preliminary governance plan that was adopted prior to opening. The preliminary governance plan was sent to the CUNY Board of Trustees in March 2012, five months before the college opened. The working committee assigned to make recommendations about governance was chaired by Associate University Provost Julia Wrigley. Under Wrigley's leadership and in consultation with Senior Vice Chancellor (SVC) for Legal Affairs Frederick Schaffer, the committee determined that absent a formal departmental structure and as a result of the heavy pedagogical demands of the institution, governance work in the start-up phase should be streamlined as much as possible.[1] Discussion at the college regarding the recommendations made by the working group spoke to the concern of the faculty regarding the absence of departmental- or program-level organization. The conflict over academic departments appeared in many conversations over the course of the planning phase and many years into the college's operation, but from the standpoint of governance, mixed messages were given with regard to why departments and chairs were non-negotiable with the administration. In one instance, SVC Frederick Schaffer remarked that the chancellor and the board of trustees would not look favorably on the college if it decided to adopt departments since the focus of the small institution was on interdisciplinary teaching and learning.[2] A similar rationale was offered by consultant Larry Mucciolo. Mucciolo suggested that the college may, at some point, decide to adopt a program coordinator or departmental structure but the faculty should be primarily focused on operationalizing the integrative FYE.[3] One faculty member inquired as to who would maintain personnel files and assist faculty in reappointment, promotion, and tenure proceedings. The administration stated that the provost would attend to these matters.

In addition to discussion involving the college's organizational structure, members of the working committee on governance paid specific attention to how aspects of a faculty member's contribution to the college would weigh in personnel decisions. The preliminary document outlining the reappointment, promotion, and tenure procedures identified teaching effectiveness as the most critical point of evaluation in a faculty member's record. Commitment to the innovative model, utilizing HIPS, and providing consistent feedback and evaluation were detailed as effective teaching practices in the Reappointment, Promotion, and Tenure (RPT) document.[4] During Guttman's first year in operation, though, there were not enough tenured faculty members to serve on the college's personnel committee. Laura Gambino was the only faculty member who was hired with tenure. A decision was made to allow tenured consortial faculty members, faculty who had tenure at other CUNY campuses and had participated in the planning of the new college, to serve on a special personnel committee until such time as there were enough tenured permanent faculty members at Guttman to constitute a personnel committee.

Although this structure was necessary, it furthered the anxiety of the founding faculty with regard to their own professional development. Since the special personnel committee was primarily comprised of tenured faculty from other colleges, faculty at Guttman were being evaluated through a range of different lenses not germane to the context in which they taught. Also, the committee was working with a preliminary evaluation rubric that delivered mixed signals regarding what was considered adequate progress in the category of research. The initial RPT document suggested that the definition of research be broad and include the oft-discussed but ill-defined scholarship of teaching and learning.[5] Some faculty believed this definition of research to include the development of Guttman's innovative model. Although there is no written evidence to suggest that this was established as a uniform policy, it emerged as a shared belief among founding faculty. The preliminary RPT document lacked specificity and instead suggests that faculty produce scholarship in their fields, as well as in areas of teaching and learning.[6] This lack of guidance in the RPT document combined with a set of predominantly external peer reviewers created a frustrating evaluation process for many faculty members.

Shared Governance

The provisional governance plan called for a college council that included all full-time faculty members and the consortial faculty. In addition, the composition of the council included representatives of various divisions of the college and two students. The council was to be chaired by the president and included other members of senior staff and the college's provost. The purpose of the council was to approve necessary academic matters, hold committee elections, and advance the mission of the college through policy and personnel decisions.[7] The governance plan called for three standing committees: (1) Curriculum and Student Academic Support Committee, (2) Agenda Committee, and (3) Assessment and Professional Development Committee. The interim governance plan also included the college personnel committee and the special personnel committee.[8] Under this plan, the college council acted as a committee-of-the-whole and included all faculty. For several years, while the college's instructional staff remained quite small, this approach was satisfactory. However, after several rounds of intensive hiring between 2012 and 2015, it became acutely apparent that a more representative approach was required.

Work on Guttman's new governance plan began in earnest in 2015 and concluded two years later in May 2017. The task force on governance was composed of elected faculty representatives and appointed administrators and staff members from each of the college's major divisions. The task force was jointly chaired by Professors Alia Tyner-Mullings and Sebastien Buttet. The charge of the task force was to submit a proposed governance plan for review by the college community and the CUNY Board of Trustees. The task force supported the idea that the college council be representative, consisting of faculty, staff, and students, all of whom would be voted onto council in staggered terms. The issue of representation, however, raised a separate set of concerns with regard to how faculty would be organized on the council. Since President Evenbeck and many members of the faculty remained committed to the absence of academic departments, the governance task force explored ways to arrange the faculty into disciplinary groupings so that the council included a diverse membership. This conversation addressed not only how the membership of the college council would be organized but also the idea of disciplinary groupings provided the opportunity for a more refined reappointment, promotion, and tenure apparatus. The task force settled on three practice areas within which faculty would be assigned based on their disciplinary expertise: (1) social sciences, (2) humanities, and (3) STEM. This approach allowed for the disciplines to be uniformly represented on the council and provide a potential additional layer to the personnel process. The task force agreed that the lack of disciplinary representation on the college personnel committee presented problems for the review process. It was difficult for faculty from contrasting disciplines to adequately evaluate research in an unfamiliar area. With this in mind, the task force proposed the creation of a tiered approach to the personnel process, with a meta-major faculty personnel committee serving as the initial reviewers of reappointment, promotion, and tenure packages.

The task force faced another key decision with regard to the creation of a representative faculty body. The majority of CUNY campuses had some form of a faculty senate. The CUNY bylaws article 2.8 call for the establishment of a University Faculty Senate. The colleges, as part of the larger university system, typically have a similar body to represent faculty concerns. Guttman, however, did not believe that a body composed only of faculty was consistent with its mission to break down the barriers between collegiate divisions. Instead, the task force imagined a representative body designed to take up academic issues but one that included administrative and support staff, as well as faculty. There were concerns by some members of the task force that administrative participation in this body would attempt to silence faculty concerns. However, the majority of the task force argued that if a senate were to be proposed it must be in line with Guttman's values of collaboration and transparency. Ultimately, the governance task force settled on an Academic Senate. The role of the senate was to facilitate conversation about matters related to the academic enterprise. Although the senate did not have a formal role in approving policy decisions recommended by the standing committees of the council, it provided a space within which debate about such matters could occur. Since the adoption of the formal governance plan in 2017, the Academic Senate has made substantial strides in forming its unique identity in the college's infrastructure. Over the past two years, the senate has provided critical feedback on issues related to remediation, the composition of the FYE, and student financial aid.

The most significant challenge this college has faced with regard to shared governance is the labor-intensive model the task force proposed. Representation on each standing committee, council, senate, and personnel committees required the full commitment of faculty and staff.

Many faculty and staff members serve on multiple committees and spend a substantial part of the workweek engaged in shared governance activities. The governance task force designed the plan for a much larger college, believing that the institution was poised for significant growth in the coming years. However, this belief has not yet come to pass, and the college is overburdened by the demands of the governance structure. Once the college is in a place where enrollment can grow, the number of faculty and staff added to support these additional students will allow for the current governance plan to proceed without placing such a heavy demand on faculty and staff. The conclusion of this chapter will discuss alternatives to the approach Guttman took in developing its governance plan.

Accreditation

Guttman Community College was awarded accreditation by the New York State Board of Regents in December 2012. In 2014, the college prepared for its first external accreditation by the Middle States Commission on Higher Education (Middle States). Over the course of two years, Guttman faculty and administrators constructed a comprehensive self-study to address the commission's 14 standards. Under the direction of Dean of Strategic Planning and Accreditation Stuart Cochran and math professor Rebecca Walker, the college highlighted what it believed to be successful elements of the unique academic enterprise. There were key areas in the self-study that members of the Middle States team, which visited the college in 2017, believed were inadequately addressed in the current operational structure. The team required Guttman to address its concerns and file a monitoring report a year later identifying how changes had been made to the current structure.

The Middle States team stated that the college's commitment to professional development should be strengthened. The self-study did not effectively detail how institutional resources were being allocated to professional development. During the 2017–2018 year, however, the college made substantial revisions to its professional development plan. Guttman made substantial improvements in the area of human resources. New faculty onboarding, updated personnel review processes, and a three-part management leadership training were developed in response recommendations made by the Middle States team.[9] In 2018, Guttman launched an implicit bias training series led by the Equity, Diversity, and Inclusion Taskforce. Faculty, staff, and administration participated in the first of a series of daylong training exercises with Jonathan Poullard, president of the California-based Equity Consulting Group. This professional development series coincided with workshops on positive classroom dynamics and neurodiversity.[10] Senior leadership indicated that it planned to generate a professional calendar to better organize workshops and seminars for the community.

The Middle States team indicated several areas where Guttman could refine assessment processes. Under Laura Gambino's leadership, learning outcomes and program assessment at Guttman were largely underway by the time of the site visit but several key processes required additional attention. First, it was recommended that faculty and administrators work to uniformly align course learning outcomes on syllabi. This process formalized course learning outcomes across all sections and prompted faculty to organize course content around a uniform set of goals. Second, the Middle States team recommended the college develop more comprehensive signature assignments for the first year and programs of study. Although the process was poised to take multiple years to implement, the work to construct such assignments began in earnest in spring 2017 with the launch of a signature assignment professional development workshop organized by the Assessment and Professional Development Committee. One of the central concerns raised in the accreditation process was how the FYE should be assessed since it was not a formal program of study. The understanding was that even though the FYE was represented by a series of courses and had multiple individuals supervising its operations, direct assessment of student learning should be handled in the same way, through the evaluation of signature assignments, as the programs of study.[11]

One substantive change that emerged from the initial accreditation process was how students moved through the quantitative reasoning and mathematics tracks at Guttman. Data indicated that over 60% of students completed the required math sequence of quantitative reasoning and statistics within the first year and over 70% completed the same track within two years.[12] In response to these data, the college adjusted the formula by which students were assigned to the one-semester versus yearlong statistics course. Recognizing that high school performance is a better predictor of student learning outcomes in college, the Guttman administration decided to include a student's secondary school GPA as a major criterion for determining the appropriate statistics track. Additionally, the number of contact hours for the yearlong statistics course was reduced by 30 minutes per week.[13] Assessment of student learning in the math program at Guttman continued in the subsequent two years, attempting to remedy stubbornly low pass rates in the yearlong statistics course. At the time of writing, there is a campus-wide conversation around the relevance of the quantitative reasoning component of City Seminar. Dialogue is specifically related to the need for such extensive hours in mathematics, especially for students who enroll proficient in basic skills. A later chapter will discuss this in more detail.

In 2016, the college convened a working group to evaluate the impact and effectiveness of the City Seminar course. At first, the central issue the group was to take up was regarding the retake sections of the course. Students who were not successful in City Seminar on their first attempt have historically been required to retake the course with other unsuccessful students in the subsequent long semester. Participation rates, classroom management, and outcomes in these sections have long been problematic. One reason such issues occur in retake City Seminar courses is that students are stigmatized and separated from their peers. Instead of allowing unsuccessful students to enroll in a regular section of City Seminar, it has been college policy to create separate sections for these students rather than contaminate the cohort structure of the first year with external students. On all levels, this arrangement has not worked. The City Seminar working group met through the 2016–2017 academic year, and by 2018, issued a set of recommendations to the college about how to overhaul the course. One of the critical decisions made by this team was the elimination of the required reading and writing component of City Seminar. This decision emerged from an earlier study comparing the outcomes of students at Guttman to a similar group of students in CUNY's ASAP program. The findings indicated that students at Guttman who failed one of the first-year courses were less likely to re-enroll and complete the course compared to ASAP students. One such rationale for this was that Guttman courses required students to complete the full set of 10.5 hours per week in order to satisfy the requirement for City Seminar. Moreover, over 70% of students at Guttman enrolled at the college proficient in reading and writing. These combined data points suggested that the high volume of contact hours for City Seminar was a hindrance to student success rather than supportive of academic outcomes.[14] The decision to eliminate reading and writing reduced the number of required hours in City Seminar, setting the college up to take on additional reductions to support student success and provide equitable learning opportunities for all students.

The Middle States team strongly encouraged the college to revise its policies and processes for reappointment, promotion, and tenure. These procedures had, along with the college's interim governance plan, been provisionally adopted, but their utility to support faculty had passed the point of expiration. Under the leadership of then English professor Nicola Blake, a team of faculty and administration engaged in a wholesale revision of the RPT document. Blake and her team worked to streamline the annual process, providing clear pathways through each personnel decision that included interfacing with the new faculty personnel committees for each academic practice area. Additionally, clarifications were made to once confusing expectations around research and service. Clear distinctions were made for faculty about what was expected at each stage of their tenure track. Blake and her team put forward a revised document that not only spelled out the requirements for reappointment, promotion, and tenure but also clearly detailed how each stage of the process functioned, complete with predictable deadlines and ways to gain support and mentorship to ensure success.

Lessons for Higher Education

Phased-In Governance

One of the most critical lessons from the Guttman Community College story is the importance of considering a phased-in approach for governance for new institutions. In response to the community's call for a more effective and organized governance plan, the college lurched from the provisional framework to a plan that could serve a large, mature college. Although this was done for the right reasons, it was, in retrospect, misguided. The faculty and staff felt that the provisional governance plan was cumbersome for a college with a larger staff. For example, requiring all faculty to serve on the college council was no longer feasible since faculty ranks had grown to over 50. However, in an effort to make a more representative body, the new permanent governance plan required full participation from the college community to fill the requisite spots on each committee and governing body. Certainly, the provisional plan was cumbersome, but the new governance plan failed to account for the current size of the institution and instead imagined an institution with more students, more staff, and more space. Rather, Guttman should have taken a phased-in approach to governance. The committee may have considered a strategic plan for college governance, one that reached thresholds of committee participation over five or ten years. These thresholds would have been aligned with potential increases in student enrollment and, thus, increases in staffing levels. The value in such an approach would have been the college's ability to hold at a certain phase if growth was delayed or did not materialize. Since the governance task force anticipated the college would be awarded a permanent physical plant by the university in the near term, it predicted that a fully operational committee structure would be needed to support the institution. However, it became clear in the years to follow that there were no plans for the college to grow and that the central office was not prepared to allocate space elsewhere for Guttman. This meant that student enrollment would be flat for the indefinite future and, as a result, the college would not be able to hire additional faculty or staff. Yet Guttman is saddled with a fully operational governance structure that is burdensome for faculty and staff. Although participation is strong, maintaining the integrity of the committees and governing bodies is labor intensive and unsustainable at the current operational capacity. Shrinking budgets and the potential for reduced enrollment as the result of the current COVID-19 pandemic will put additional strain on the college's governance processes. A phased-in approach would have permitted the college to hold steady at a particular level until such a time as growth was necessary.

Too Much, Too Fast

In an effort to be enthusiastically innovative, Guttman Community College adopted a full range of experimental initiatives that it attempted to operationalize all at once. Intrusive advising, learning communities, HIPS, and an interdisciplinary FYE were expected to launch simultaneously and work well. Guttman's initial experience with accreditation underscored critical areas of college operations that were undernourished as a result of the rapid pace at which the model was launched. When the college was founded, assessment, both institutional and outcomes, was its operational backbone. The plans for ongoing, in-depth, and campus-wide assessment of the educational model were necessary in order for Guttman to effectively alter its practices to enhance student performance. In the rush to fully implement all of the experimental components of the model, it became clear very early on that the accelerated pace of opening prevented the college from establishing a systematic and informative assessment plan. For example, the CCE was designed to be the hub of assessment work for the institution. However, leadership missteps were made in the first year that stunted the development of the CCE. The senior staff determined that the CCE would be jointly managed by Laura Gambino and newly hired CCE director Elisa Hertz. The two disagreed over responsibilities, which stalled the organization of a clear assessment protocol. This left the college without much knowledge of itself and flying blind with regard to the effectiveness of the model. In order for the full model to be implemented from the start, a bold venture by itself, the college would have benefited from a rigorous and systematic plan for evaluation. For many reasons, an external research organization, such as MDRC or Ithaka S + R, would have been an excellent option to provide an objective analysis of the institution.

Notes

1. Notes from the New Community College New Committee Meeting, February 17, 2012.
2. Notes, February 17, 2012.
3. Notes, February 17, 2012.
4. Notes from the Reappointment, Promotion, and Tenure Taskforce, September 2012.
5. Notes, September 2012.
6. Notes, September 2012.
7. New Community College at CUNY, *New Community College Interim Governance Plan*, August 29, 2012.
8. New Community College at CUNY, 4.
9. Stella and Charles Guttman Community College, *Monitoring Report to the Middle States Commission on Higher Education* (New York, NY: Stella and Charles Guttman Community College, August 30, 2018).
10. Stella and Charles Guttman Community College, 9.
11. Stella and Charles Guttman Community College, 12.
12. Stella and Charles Guttman Community College, 13.
13. Stella and Charles Guttman Community College, 13.
14. Charles R. Jordan, "Exploring Shifting Moments of Remediation: An Analysis of Developmental Education Policies at the City University of New York" (PhD diss., City University of New York, 2017).

4   Curricular Challenges

As Guttman Community College moved from start-up mode into a longer period of institutional maturation, the innovative curriculum emerged as the central source of conflict for members of the community. Early data showed flagging mathematics outcomes, poor transfer performance, and alumni survey evidence consistently faulted the college for inadequate preparation. These performance metrics mixed with a recognition that the additional contact hours required of all students were ineffective at nurturing healthy academic outcomes and were instead vestiges of the racial and socioeconomic assumptions made in the concept paper. However, as this chapter will detail, these data were not enough to radically refocus the curriculum. There remained vocal elements of the community that actively resisted restructuring the educational model, even though its apparent inequities in outcomes persisted. This was especially true with regard to transfer. Poor transfer outcomes were the first indication that the Guttman model did not satisfactorily prepare students for continued postsecondary work. However, many looked for alternative explanations.

The FYE Revisited

Since before the college opened, the hallmark of the institution was the FYE. Intensive planning and hours of intellectual labor went into developing courses like City Seminar and Ethnographies of Work. Although Guttman was designed to be responsive to its data, the way in which the FYE was constructed made it difficult to revise. The interlocking components of City Seminar, each taught by an individual faculty member in a rigid course timetable, were so fused together that restructuring one element meant the entire course had to be redesigned. Also, Guttman's small size was financially compensated by the additional contact hours in the FYE. Each of the required contact hours earned the college full-time equivalents. Until the college could substantially grow its enrollment numbers, this approach kept the institution financially solvent. However, there were early indications, even prior to data on transfer became available, that pointed to trouble for the FYE.

Even in the first year the college was open, the structure of the FYE triggered problems for the institution. The learning community model designed to foster relationships within a cohort immediately led to classroom management issues. The effects of hyper-bonding, where individuals develop a group mentality resulting from excessive time spent together, became increasingly prevalent across the FYE Houses. Faculty and advising staff faced challenging classroom dynamics. In some cases, an entire cohort's success was diminished by a core group of disengaged or misbehaved students. In other cases, high-performing students were frustrated by their cohort's immaturity. On most college campuses, students develop from the immaturity of high school to a more mature self as they navigate new relationships and experiences in the first year of college. The Guttman first-year model stunts that development by forcing students into communal classroom experiences, preventing them from creating their own adult relationships with a diverse group of peers. For some students, this environment perpetuates the milieu of high school, and for others, it serves as a crushing reminder that they are not party to a normal collegiate experience, a rite of passage for many young people.

This disruptive classroom environment is perpetuated in weekly faculty/staff instructional team meetings. The instructional team was designed as a space within which faculty and advising staff meet to discuss student performance and engage in assessment of student work. Instead, these meetings often evolved into spaces that perpetuate the deficit-laden assumptions about student ability. Although conversations at these meetings vary from team to team and certainly do not all approach student learning from the same negative mindset, the manner by which these teams are organized lends itself to generalizations and implicit bias. There are myriad examples of teams recognizing poor student performance and then attempting to problematize it or find the root cause of disengagement. These reasons, all of which have been discussed publicly at the college, include a student's problems at home, parenting struggles, food insecurity, legal troubles, work/school imbalance, mental illness, and learning disabilities. Certainly, all of these are real issues students face. And many students at Guttman and CUNY face one or more of these challenges. That, however, is not the concern here. The continuing problem in the instructional team model is that faculty, none of whom are experts in any of these areas, make presumptive leaps to these highly racialized topics in an attempt to explain poor academic performance.

Although this is not the case uniformly, it has been an evolving and consistent trope emerging from the instructional team meetings. These presumptions layer onto the cultural narrative of the concept paper and have made it difficult to move beyond an institutional perspective of Guttman students as underachieving and underprepared for college work. However, the model itself created a space where faculty would engage with students beyond just classroom teaching, leaving them susceptible to bias and presumption.

There are many problems associated with deficit narratives about students in a collegiate setting. A central concern is that if a culture of inability and underpreparedness are ascribed to a student population, then the presumption is that academic standards will be lowered to meet these perceived shortcomings. Since Guttman Community College was charged with substantially raising completion rates but organized around a culture of inability, data should point to red flags in student performance metrics. And they most certainly do. One study illustrates this through a comparison of Guttman student outcomes by entering proficiency status. By the end of the FYE, remedial and nonremedial students earn relatively the same mean GPA. However, by the end of the following year, after students have taken courses in their elected major, the outcomes between the two groups diverge sharply, with nonremedial students outperforming remedial students by 0.2 GPA points. There are a number of explanations for this divergence that are distinctly tied to the first-year courses. Guttman policy is that students cannot earn a failing grade on their first attempt at courses in the FYE. Instead, unsuccessful students earn a grade of NC, which does not impact their GPA and allows them to retake the course without academic penalty. Although Guttman does not track students into courses based on entering remedial status, this marker of proficiency is a way to distinguish how students perform compared to one another. Traditionally, remedial students underperform compared to their nonremedial peers. Since there is no failing grade option for the FYE courses at Guttman, the grades of poorly performing students are artificially inflated. This makes it difficult to distinguish how effective the FYE is at providing developmental skills remediation. Yet as students move from the FYE into their respective majors where grades and instruction follow a more traditional format, the distinction between remedial students and nonremedial students emerges with regard to performance. This is a possible indicator that the FYE is ineffective at providing students with the fundamental skills they need to be successful in the long run, even though they are required to enroll in an exceedingly high number of contact hours to remedy basic skills deficits.

Another issue with these data points suggests that the FYE continues to perpetuate the stigma of remediation. Rather than raising the bar, as college courses should, the FYE exacerbates the culture of low standards that is commonplace in city high schools. In order to break that cycle, Guttman students should be introduced to challenging coursework that welcomes them into the academy. And enrollment data further that argument even more. Entering student proficiency data indicated that over 70% of freshmen at Guttman enrolled into the FYE already proficient in reading and writing. However, students were required to, as part of City Seminar, take three hours of zero-credit reading and writing developmental education per week in the first semester. Although this course was not a traditional zero-credit developmental class, it was a component of City Seminar that required student participation regardless of proficiency status. This policy did not, however, align with student data. Guttman was designed to be responsive to student enrollment and outcome metrics and to be flexible enough to adjust the curriculum accordingly. However, as the years progressed, attempts to address misalignments in the curriculum were met with staunch opposition by a core group of faculty members. The group of faculty members who argued against changing the model believed students needed the extra hours in class to do well, and later a new rationale evolved stating that the additional contact hours were necessary to do integrative teaching and learning well. Yet the original purpose for the additional contact hours in City Seminar was to provide additional time for developmental skills to be integrated into college-level coursework. However, the assumptions regarding entering student proficiency levels were discredited by years of data that showed Guttman enrolling a higher percentage of proficient students than the planning team imagined. The college's unwillingness to change indicated that assumptions about student ability were firmly ingrained into the culture of the institution.

As new members joined the Guttman community and approached the first-year curriculum with a critical eye, these assumptions began to be challenged. What became abundantly clear was that continuing to mandate students of all proficiency levels enroll in 10.5 hours of coursework for which they only earned three credits was inequitable. And the assumptions that kept this structure afloat were very recognizably based on presumptions of race and social class. Against staunch opposition from some faculty, Provost Wach called for the removal of the reading and writing component from City Seminar, citing the high percentage of students entering Guttman with proficiency in reading and writing as evidence for change. Wach worked with English faculty to shift the three-credit Composition 1 course to the fall semester so that students would have the opportunity to earn additional college credits earlier in their freshman year. To support students who required additional hours of developmental education in reading and writing by university standards, Wach and the faculty adopted a corequisite model where nonproficient students would enroll into Composition 1 and a weekly supplemental instructional section that offered additional skills-building exercises. Some members of the community strongly believed that more needed to be done to reduce the number of contact hours required in City Seminar.

Conversations about implicit bias and institutional racism emerged during Wach's tenure as provost. Under the leadership of Dr. Lavita McMath Turner, the college grappled with its roots and its cultural fabric. What was clear for many, though not all, was that the institution, and especially the FYE, had to change to ensure students were receiving a rigorous education that prepared them for transfer. Because the FYE was the college's central site for remediation and where disparities in outcomes were distinctly observable, conflict between a fundamentalist group of faculty members who wanted to protect the original concept and those who demanded change dominated the political landscape at Guttman. Faculty, staff, and administration participated in hours of implicit bias training and attended workshops on culturally relevant pedagogy. Throughout this, though, the FYE remained the same. After the reading and writing component was removed, there was continued evidence to suggest that the additional hours in math were unneeded and that the quantitative reasoning component of City Seminar should be removed. Students satisfied their math proficiency requirements in the statistics course, yet every freshman was required to attend quantitative reasoning for three hours per week for the entire first year for which they received no college credit. With over 50% of students entering Guttman already proficient in math, the expectation that all students enroll in a yearlong, noncredit section of quantitative reasoning was excessive. However, the institution did not respond to these data points. Instead, the college continued to acquiesce to a convincing math faculty with regard to the efficacy of quantitative reasoning. Although math leadership did not have data showing the value of the additional hours, it continued as part of City Seminar. For some members of the Guttman Community, these curricular practices that flew in the face of current data represented an affront to equity in education. Continuing to enroll students, regardless of their entering performance metrics, into remedial coursework was disproportionately harming students of color who made up the predominance of Guttman's population.

The Programs of Study

Since opening, the college's five programs of study evolved and developed unique identities within the institutional community. Unlike the FYE, each of the majors introduced students to a more traditional college education. The college took a drastically different approach to the programs of study than was envisioned in the concept paper. The planning phase began in earnest during the height of the Great Recession and influenced how the team constructed the proposed set of 12 majors. The initial programs of study were to be vocational in nature and highly specialized. They included fields such as nursing, surgical technology, and supply chain management. However, space and financial restrictions quickly eliminated these skilled majors from consideration. Instead, the college opened in 2012 with six programs of study. The liberal arts and sciences (LAS) major quickly became the program with the highest enrollment. This trend was in line with CUNY's community college enrollment data that showed over 30% of students enrolled in a LAS associate's degree program. At Guttman, the LAS major introduced students to courses in disciplines such as sociology, anthropology, English, and physical sciences. As information on student transfer became readily available, there was interest among LAS faculty to develop tracks within the major to better prepare students for specific baccalaureate disciplines. Faculty created a science track within the LAS major and are planning to implement a social science and humanities track in the coming year.

In response to Guttman's first accreditation, each of the programs of study organized an advisory board of external partners who served as academic and industry mentors to faculty as they continued to develop their programs. Urban Studies Program Coordinator Molly Makris included city agency leaders, organization executives, and prominent academics, each of whom offered a unique perspective on the kinds of urban issues students discussed in the classroom. Information Technology Program Coordinator Dalvin Hill successfully partnered with the New York–based Per Scholas to provide students with a pathway for credentialing and certification in computer programming. These efforts opened multiple avenues for students who sought to transfer to a four-year college or shift directly into the workplace.

Assessment Days

One of the hallmarks of Guttman's unique educational model was the college's ten assessment days. Each academic year, ten calendar days were set aside for faculty and staff to meet for daylong activities related to student learning assessment. The concept paper called for an institutional culture of rigorous assessment, both of student learning outcomes and institutional operations. The college hired Laura Gambino partly because of her experience with assessment using ePortfolios as the mechanism by which faculty and staff evaluated student learning. During the college's first year, Gambino began to work with faculty and staff to initiate the first assessment cycle. Each of the first-year courses identified a series of signature assignments that were uniform across all sections. These assignments, ranging from term papers to creative projects and presentations were uploaded into each student's ePortfolio and captured by the software system's assessment tool. Gambino organized the first assessment days so that faculty could use a preliminary learning outcomes rubric to evaluate student work. For most faculty, this was a new and unfamiliar process. Many on the instructional staff had little experience teaching full time, and even fewer had direct experience with assessment. Over the course of two days, Gambino led faculty through norming processes, technology tutorials, and evaluation of student work. The college expected all faculty to participate fully in each day's activities.

Throughout the first year, it became clear that the evolution of assessment at Guttman would be piecemeal. Faculty and administration quickly realized that the college needed to adopt its own set of learning outcomes that reflected the culture of the institution and its courses. During the spring semester, a core group of faculty members, led by Gambino, participated in a multi-day retreat to construct what would become the GLOs. The GLOs reflected the style and substance learning outcomes rubrics that had become popular during the recession era at colleges across the country. They included categories such as broad, integrative knowledge; intellectual skills; and civic engagement. Faculty and staff began to utilize the GLOs in 2013 during assessment days. Gambino and the Assessment and Professional Development Committee organized a multiyear assessment cycle to evaluate student learning using each of the GLO rubrics. Faculty interested in assessment volunteered to serve on one of several GLO teams, whose responsibility it was to evaluate student work and help the college to understand the effectiveness of the rubric for their assigned GLO. The process indicated that, although the GLOs were designed to reflect the work being done at Guttman, the results did not adequately capture student learning in a way that was meaningful and actionable. Instead, the GLO team assessment work underscored the critical need for revision in the area of learning outcomes assessment.

Since its beginning, the assessment days at Guttman have evolved. Requiring a much larger faculty to participate in several multi-day assessment activities throughout the year is both unsustainable and unscalable.

Instead, the faculty and staff leaders have developed these days into professional development opportunities for the entire community that are grounded in key areas of institutional effectiveness and learning outcomes assessment. Assessment days still include opportunities for faculty to engage with direct assessment of student work but are interspersed with other activities.

Community Days

While faculty and staff participated in assessment days, students, especially those in the first year, signed up for mandatory community days activities. Community days were designed to give students an opportunity to do service-learning projects in the New York City metro area. Ideally, these projects were to be connected to the theme of the City Seminar. During the early years of the college, students were assigned to projects in the city by House. These projects included performing volunteer cleanup in Bryant Park, assisting on urban farms, and participating in soup kitchens across the city. The intention of community days was to directly connect the curriculum to the lives of those living in New York. Over time, however, activities varied more than they did in Guttman's formative years and included seminars and professional development opportunities with local business leaders. Some members of the Guttman community raised concerns about having students perform manual labor tasks during community days activities, signaling that such assignments could be racialized if not grounded in an appropriate context. Another key issue was that students were required to participate in activities that stretched beyond normal contact hours for their first-year courses, calling into question the ethics of community days.

Arts in New York City

The Arts in New York City is a required general education course for students at Guttman. The concept for the arts course was to introduce students to a variety of artistic traditions and to expose students to the wide array of cultural institutions in New York City. Shortly after the course launched, faculty worked to incorporate resident artists who spent a week or more in the classroom with students focused on a specific art form. One example included Peter Kyle, who worked with several classes of students on forms of modern dance. Kyle structured his classes in such a way that students felt comfortable exploring an artistic form that required both concentration and vulnerability around their peers. Students also were able to spend a good deal of time traveling to locations outside of the classroom.

Over the eight years the course ran, students were required to visit the Metropolitan Museum of Art on Manhattan's Fifth Avenue. The Met does not mandate an entrance fee for local visitors but does require payment for groups and tours. To avoid having students pay for a group rate, faculty encouraged students to travel independently to the Met or with a small group of friends. At one point in the fall 2019 semester, a group of Guttman students was stopped by Met security and questioned about what they were doing at the museum. At the college, this was cause for alarm. Institutions across New York City were actively focused on building more equitable workplaces, directly confronting systemic forms of institutional racism that continued to disproportionately impact communities of color. The interaction between the Met security and Guttman students was another instance of this. Faculty, students, and administration alerted Met leadership, who quickly organized a meeting for the involved parties. In an honest dialogue, the Met shared that it was continuing to examine its own culture of racial bias and vowed to work closely with the college to establish a more trustworthy relationship.

Additionally, there were concerns regarding the academic efficacy of the arts course. Across the various sections of the course, there were drastically different requirements for the quality of student work and participation. Pass rates were incredibly high but there was limited understanding at the institutional level on how the arts course prepared students civically or academically. Guttman faculty valued the exposure students received with regard to the various trips out of the classroom, but some wondered whether such exposure was academically satisfactory. At the time of writing, there are ongoing debates in various committees at Guttman on how best to revise the arts course. Some options on the table include broadening the types of cultural institutions students interact with throughout the course so that such exposure is culturally relevant, safe, and academically rigorous. Others involve including a more focused engagement with art history so that students are prepared to enter a four-year college readied with information relative to cultural history both in New York City and globally. There are preparations to introduce a new faculty expert who can assist in developing a revised curriculum for the Arts in New York City course.

Transfer

According to recent survey data, over 85% of Guttman students expressed a desire to transfer to a four-year college. Many of these students hoped to begin their college journeys in a baccalaureate program but were unable to meet the baseline entrance requirements or could not afford the cost. For them, community college was a backup option, one they wanted to move through quickly. At CUNY, scores of community college students seeking a bachelor's degree are mandated to begin at the community colleges because they lack proficiency in one or more basic skills. This policy, created in 2000, prevents students from enrolling at one of the four-year colleges until such remedial requirements are successfully completed. Scores of students fail to complete these required zero-credit sequences and/or deplete critical financial aid funds in the process, leaving them unable to transfer and earn a bachelor's degree. Guttman Community College was, in part, designed to eliminate the ubiquitous use of zero-credit remedial courses. The embedded developmental skills model of the FYE was intended to increase the number of hours students spent in a credit-bearing, college-level course without the stigma of being in remediation. This shift in practice opened the door for many more students to begin earning college credits from the time of matriculation and has largely contributed to the college's high graduation rates. Yet the model did not meet its objectives. Guttman instead reconfigured the traditional zero-credit model and applied the remedial stigma to the entire student population which, in turn, lowered the standard of academic excellence and furthered inequities.

Although Guttman graduated far more students than its peer colleges, early data indicated that students who graduated from Guttman and transferred to a four-year CUNY college were struggling to succeed. This drop in GPA between a student's last semester at the community college and the first two semesters at the four-year college is known as transfer shock. In comparison to a group of students with similar characteristics from a peer CUNY institution, Guttman students transferred in higher numbers but performed markedly lower in the first two semesters after transfer. In fact, the highest performing Guttman students, those with superior GPAs and those who graduated in two years, fared the worst once they transferred. There are a number of possible explanations for this phenomenon, all of which have been discussed extensively by Guttman faculty, staff, and administration.

First, the intensive student support model, small class sizes, and focus on relationship building is not replicable at expansive four-year colleges. CUNY four-year colleges are largely traditional academic institutions. Students are expected to navigate layered bureaucracies in the academic, financial, and student support domains. Unlike Guttman, the four-year colleges, apart from a range of special programs, do not organize students into learning communities and have not invested in the types of advising structures that permit professional staff to establish close, personal relationships with students. The shift from the tightly structured

Guttman environment to one that mandates individual independence can disrupt student learning and overall performance. Second, the disjuncture between the learning experience at Guttman and that of the four-year colleges is stark. Guttman's curriculum, especially in the first year, is devoid of traditional academic content and rather fueled by interdisciplinary group projects that are drawn from a core set of urban issues. Faculty at Guttman privilege presentations, papers, and creative projects over exams. However, as many students have reported, the nontraditional curriculum does not effectively prepare them for the rigors of baccalaureate study. Lastly, Guttman is still in the process of creating strong transfer partnerships with four-year institutions. One of the critical components of the concept paper was how the programs of study would develop articulation agreements with CUNY baccalaureate programs. At present, program coordinators are working with the university through the auspices of the BTAG and with individual departments to ensure that Guttman students are adequately supported with regard to credit transfer once they are accepted to a four-year college.

Discussions around transfer at Guttman have raised a number of concerns that are directly related to the dialogue around race and equity at the institution. Guttman's first look at transfer data revealed potential problems with the model. Although graduation rates remained high in the first eight years of the college's operations, Guttman transfer students had the lowest mean transfer GPA in the system. Since the number of students who have transferred from Guttman represents only a small fraction of the total number of transfer students at CUNY, the poor performance of this population of transfer students raised red flags for some faculty and staff at Guttman. At Guttman, conversations centered on academic preparation. Certainly, faculty and staff recognized that there were variables for which they could not entirely control, including how four-year colleges received transfer students. In many cases, as new studies are showing, the ways in which receiving colleges support transfer students is widely varied and often lacking in basic onboarding practices such as orientation and advising. However, community colleges also have the responsibility to prepare students academically for successful transfer. The critical piece of data that indicated to Guttman faculty and staff that curricular changes were necessary to better facilitate transfer was the steep post-transfer GPA of high-performing Guttman students. This indicated that Guttman students were prepared to do well at Guttman but that the academic rigor of the college's programs needed to be revised to support long-term academic health.

Guttman had to understand the concept of transfer within the context of CUNY history. Since the 2000 decision to eliminate transfer at the four-year colleges, the percentage of White students in the community colleges declined as the number of students of color, particularly those identifying as Hispanic, increased substantially. However, survey data show that the large majority of community college students hope to attain a bachelor's degree and would have preferred to begin at a four-year college. Barriers like remediation, the use of standardized test scores in admissions processes, and availability of financial aid prevent students of color from enrolling directly into four-year institutions. In turn, the community college experience, rife with curricular and bureaucratic challenges, acts as a deterrent to bachelor's attainment. To undo patterns of racism that prevent students of color from achieving a bachelor's degree, Guttman had to provide a rigorous academic experience that challenged racial stereotypes while supporting a seamless pathway toward transfer.

Guttman was designed to be an innovative institution that facilitated student completion. The transfer mission was not recognized as a central focus for the college during its planning phase. It was assumed, based on the realities of the labor market in 2007, that far more students would seek an associate's degree as a terminal degree for a specific profession. This assumption did not materialize. It became clear during the latter years of the college's planning that the job market for associate's degree holders had all but dried up in New York City. And, although the majors were adjusted to reflect this shift, the foundational elements of the model were not effectively bifurcated to support both completion and transfer. Therefore, during the operational phase, there became a disconnect between intention and reality. Certainly, there was agreement that all students who enrolled at Guttman should have clear pathways toward graduation, but it was less clear how the curriculum supported transfer.

For students transferring within the CUNY system, the FYE courses counted toward Pathways general education requirements but not to those of bachelor's degrees. However, for those who transferred to four-year colleges outside of the system, the confusing branding of courses like City Seminar and Ethnographies of Work presented problems during credit evaluation. It was not easy to discern how such courses equated to more traditional introductory classes. Even at CUNY, students have experienced difficulty transferring some courses. For students enrolled in the stretched statistics course over the full academic year, there have been issues for individuals attempting to transfer the course as a single, three-credit unit. In terms of degree credit transfer, many of Guttman's courses transfer as electives, which largely do not benefit students when they transfer. Courses like the capstone in LAS do not have equivalent courses in more traditional bachelor's degree programs. These courses are unique to Guttman.

Lessons for Higher Education

Rigorous Assessment

One of the critical elements of CUNY's ASAP program and the central reason for which it has been so successful and scalable is how carefully it has been evaluated. Over the course of more than a decade, ASAP has been the product of ongoing assessment, both internally and externally. Even though Guttman Community College was conceptually designed with assessment at the center of the model, there were no coherent plans for the assessment of the academic model. The complicated interplay between the various components of the FYE, for example, was essential to producing academically prepared young people. There are lessons to be drawn from this lapse in planning.

When Guttman opened, there should have been a commitment by the college and the university to undergo an external evaluation. CUNY has long had relationships with major New York City–based research organizations like MDRC, which have provided scientifically rigorous and thoughtful evaluations to major university programs. At the time, other community colleges could have reasonably served as comparison groups to Guttman. In 2012, almost all students requiring remediation at the community colleges at CUNY, with the exception of Guttman, were required to enroll in zero-credit courses. Although a randomized controlled trial may have not been ethically possible in an open-access institution like Guttman, statistical procedures using observational data by way of quasi-experimental methods could have helped the college understand the impact of the integrative first-year program. In the absence of such data, Guttman relied solely on faculty and staff anecdotal evidence to understand the effectiveness of the educational framework.

The absence of clear institutional assessment data prevented the institution from revising the model as it had been designed to do. The planning team imagined the college being responsive to real-time data, especially data warehoused in the CCE. However, without a clear assessment plan, there were no empirical data except for key metrics related to graduation and retention. Until 2019, faculty were flying blind. Access to student performance data at the course level was largely unavailable. Most instructors were wholly unaware of how their students were performing in the courses or programs over the long run. This, coupled with no institutional-level analysis of the effectiveness of the experimental model, left the college in the dark. For several years, Guttman heralded its high three-year graduation rates as the sole marker of its success. However, as inequities in outcomes emerged by race and for transfer students, it was clear that there were areas of the academic programming that required revision.

For Guttman, however, it was unclear what these revisions were. The poor transfer data pointed to many things but together with other metrics indicated that additional attention should be paid to the rigor of Guttman's academic programs. Senior leadership struggled to craft a vision to revise the model and threats to alter certain elements became political lightning rods. Without sufficient evidence to support suggested changes, such alterations became associated with budget cuts rather than revisions necessary to support the academic health of the students. In many ways, however, the strength of the budget was endemic to many of the proposed changes. City Seminar, for one, could not sustain itself financially with more students. Vice President for Finance and Administration Mary Coleman attempted to close multiple deficit gaps in the college's budget that stemmed from overspending in the area of academic affairs. At one point in 2019, the cost per full-time equivalent was $39,000. Certainly, the institution recognized academic deficiencies in the model as it turned to data on transfer and performance by demographic, but changes to the structure were also necessary in order for the college to be financially solvent over the long run.

Had the college opened with a rigorous plan for evaluation, issues such as cost-benefit and many of the problems with the academic model may have been alleviated. Faculty and staff would have been presented with accurate, empirical data that pointed to distinct areas of the educational enterprise that required adjustment. One of the most important considerations for colleges developing new programs or for those university systems hoping to open a new institution is how to design an effective educational program that is supported and informed by a concise assessment plan. This process provides the necessary evidentiary data that affords insight into the effectiveness of the assumptions that went into the various components of the model and also calls attention to blind spots that, over time, could easily erode perceived gains. In the case of Guttman, the lack of institutional assessment data created paralysis. Faculty and staff clung to the original model because there was little available data to convince them that revisions were necessary. The politics around those who believed the model was ineffective and those who maintained commitment to it created stark divisions between members of the community.

Although curricular concerns and conflicts are endemic to institutions of higher education, some anxiety around making necessary changes can be alleviated through access to factual data. The culture of assessment that has swept through higher education over the last decade has done so on the wings of technology. Access to software systems that report real-time, course and institutional data are essential tools for faculty and administrative leaders. As Guttman gained access to credible data, leadership was able to make a case for institutional change. However, navigating the political terrain after years of absent data was challenging. Guttman would have benefited greatly from a quality assessment plan from its beginning.

5 Revising the Model

CUNY has enacted bold academic reforms in the second decade of the 21st century. Under the leadership of Executive Vice Chancellor (EVC) and University Provost Vita Rabinowitz, and continuing with her successor José Luis Cruz, CUNY adopted significant changes to developmental education, admissions standards, and transfer policy. Guttman Community College was born in a different academic era and struggled to adjust a model that coincided with outdated policy and new reforms. This chapter details critical areas of the Guttman model that require substantive revision. Efforts to reconstruct the pillars of the educational enterprise will require the college to rely on accurate and informed data now made available by the university.

Critical Areas for Revision

Remediation

At the core of the Guttman model was a commitment to reimagine remediation. As has been discussed in this book, the traditional approach to developmental education was to enroll students in layers of zero-credit courses that served as gatekeepers to credit-bearing classes. Data showed that remedial students were predominantly people of color, most of whom never completed the required sequences and dropped out long before earning enough credits to graduate. The Guttman model offered an alternative. Instead of zero-credit courses, Guttman offered an integrative approach that combined developmental skills with credit-bearing coursework in the first year. However, the assumptions that were sewn into the model cast the entire student body as remedial, assumptions drawn from racial and socioeconomic stereotypes. The City Seminar course required students to attend class for 10.5 hours per week and only awarded them three credits. In 2007, the university signed onto this rationale, believing it a viable alternative to zero-credit courses. However, CUNY has since modified its remedial practices to be more equitable and to move toward a university free of zero-credit courses.

EVC Rabinowitz oversaw broad changes to how students were assigned to developmental education courses and launched a series of initiatives aimed at increasing the number of corequisite courses at CUNY. For decades, CUNY built a massive workforce and academic infrastructure around proficiency testing in reading, writing, and mathematics. In recent history, entering students who did not place out of remediation through high school grades, SAT scores, or other standardized metrics sat for three different placement tests. For math, students completed an exam using Accuplacer software. Cut scores were altered over time to determine if those who nearly achieved a passing score would be successful in college-level math. In writing, CUNY administered the CAT-W or CUNY Assessment Test in Writing. Faculty from across the university met regularly to evaluate student writing samples, using tested rubrics to determine if the individual met the basic writing requirements. University administrators and faculty recognized deep flaws in the use of testing to determine proficiency but lacked an appropriate alternative. Under EVC Rabinowitz's leadership, Associate University Provost David Crook led a team in drafting a proficiency index, one that abandoned the testing regime in favor of a more nuanced approach to determining proficiency.

This index combines a student's overall high school grade point average with SAT scores and Regents scores to determine the student has a high probability of passing a college-level course. In math, the subject area in which most developmental students enroll and ultimately struggle, the proficiency index is divided into three areas. For students who are assessed with a score of 60 or higher on the index, colleges must allow students to enroll in a credit-bearing college course that counts for a CUNY general education requirement.[1] For those who score lower than 60, colleges can work with students to determine the best course for them to enroll in. Unlike the former approach, a score below 60 does not mean a student is automatically assigned to zero-credit remediation. Instead, they are presented with options including summer immersion programs, corequisite courses, or CUNY Start for those individuals who require deep remediation. A similar approach is taken for English. Some students at CUNY matriculate with multiple developmental needs. These students were formerly required to enroll in multiple levels of remediation in several different subject areas, which used critical financial aid dollars and slowed progress toward a degree. Under the proficiency index method, students who require multiple forms of remediation are strongly encouraged to enroll in CUNY Start or a series of corequisite courses. Under no circumstances should colleges make recommendations for students to enroll in zero-credit courses.[2] The university notes that zero-credit courses will be phased out and replaced by corequisite courses.

Since its formation, Guttman Community College was not an active participant in the conversation around remedial reform at CUNY. Because the college was built on an integrated developmental approach, there was not campus-level conversation around how best to phase out zero-credit courses since they did not exist in name. However, as reform efforts cascaded across the university, the Guttman model of developmental education was called into question. Although the institution did not enroll students into separate, zero-credit courses, the additional time on task embedded into courses like City Seminar was required of all students even though they did not earn credits for many of these hours. For most of its early history, City Seminar required all students to sit for 10.5 hours of instruction per week but only granted them three degree credits for successful completion. The other hours were billed as developmental. Under the new proficiency metrics, many more students entered CUNY proficient in basic skills. Since the proficiency metric took into account an aggregate of high school grades and standardized test scores, this measure of ability was far more nuanced than the former placement exams. However, despite these shifts in proficiency data, Guttman continued to enroll all students in City Seminar. The 2019–2020 academic year saw the first response to the rising proficiency metrics. The academic year opened with the first substantial revision to City Seminar, which eliminated the developmental reading and writing component from the course, bringing the total number of contact hours down to 7.5. At the time of writing, students are still required to enroll in six hours of instruction per week for City Seminar, for which they only earn three credits.

A great deal has been discussed in this book about the implications of requiring excess contact hours for fewer credits than students deserve. The story of City Seminar speaks to the nature of reforms that are inflexible. In attempting to break from the traditional zero-credit remedial paradigm, the planning team and then the faculty and administration of Guttman became locked into a different type of inequitable developmental model. Since the planning team did not actually break free from zero-credit coursework but rather masked it within an integrative experience, Guttman landed in a similar position as its peer institutions. The question of how to reimagine remediation and the culture of deficit that emerges from the stigma of the zero-credit developmental paradigm continues to confound the institution. The integrated components of the first-year courses at Guttman make it challenging to revise. Yet there is an approach that would differentiate how students who require remediation would receive such instruction. The college must first culturally recognize that community college students are capable of college-level work. This is not a stigma unique to Guttman but one that an experimental college designed to break down the barriers of access and opportunity can be a leader in changing.

Since Guttman was designed to increase community college completion rates, there is substantial data to illustrate how low expectations were embedded into the curriculum so that students would have a better chance of finishing. This form of social promotion has its roots in racism and has been broadly studied across American education policy. Guttman must start the process of revision by looking squarely at its students, who they are, and what they want from college. Survey information and focus group data provide a clear answer to this quandary. The planning team did not imagine that the majority of students enrolling at Guttman would want to transfer to a four-year college. In fact, the early selection of degree programs would have been well-suited for a student body aiming for professional credentials in high-tech fields like nursing. However, the recession furthered the demand for a credentialed workforce and prompted many students who may once have entered the labor market with a high school diploma or associate's degree to pursue a baccalaureate degree. Although the founding faculty at Guttman settled on five majors for the college, most of which were not listed in the concept paper, the college was not adequately prepared to be a transfer institution. Although the interdisciplinarity of the FYE promised to introduce students to a wide range of academic content areas, the remedial nature of courses like City Seminar prevented students from accessing challenging academic material. Many faculty members believed it was the responsibility of the FYE to teach academic skills rather than disciplinary or transdisciplinary content. In fact, the concept paper alludes to the belief that the case studies used for City Seminar were simply vehicles by which basic skills could be taught.

The first-year courses were not intended to fulfill a transfer mission. Although Guttman strived to be a unique institution, free of the constraints of traditional academic departments, it was situated within an institutional context that remained deeply entrenched and committed to conventional academia. The focus on developmental skills building for all Guttman students slowed intellectual maturation and stunted the process by which college students develop as independent learners. To fulfill its obligation to effectively prepare students for transfer, the college must make substantial changes to the remedial paradigm that is particular to the FYE. Along with a differentiated approach to developmental education, the FYE, and thereafter the programs of study, must expressly prepare students for transfer. To do this, Guttman does not have to acquiesce to the traditional paradigm of the four-year college but can integrate its interdisciplinary and supportive structure with a renewed focus on academic content. In practice, this looks like flipping the script so that the focus of the FYE is not solely on skills building but is rather on rigorous academic preparation. Linked courses, advising sessions, and innovative teaching practices can remain the hallmarks of the newly constructed FYE. In order to move away from the remedial stigma and racialized assumptions framed in the concept paper, faculty and administration need to make the cultural turn toward academic preparation rather than developmental skills building.

Faculty Administrative Work

At the institutional level, there is a substantial need for revision in how administrative work is handled at the small college. When the college opened, the senior administrative cadre was quite small, especially since the college determined it would not organize academic departments. However, leadership underneath the provostial level was needed in order to manage the necessary functions of the academic enterprise. Just before the college opened, new faculty were hired to partially fulfill administrative duties. Those individuals, discussed earlier in this book, laid the groundwork for how the institution would apportion its administrative duties across the college. The pattern of assigning faculty to hybrid-administrative roles required Guttman academic leadership to allocate generous reassigned time hours to annual workloads. Over the years, the instructional obligations of many more faculty members were substantially reduced to support administrative functions. These included experiential education, program leadership, assessment and technology, Global Guttman, accreditation leadership, institutional review board coordination, and instructional team participation. These activities, all of which supported the educational model, greatly reduced the full-time teaching capacity at the college.

Over time, the stability of the FYE instructional teams was challenged by the college's inability to assign full-time faculty to each of the Houses. To preserve educational continuity and to effectively integrate academic content across all sections of a House, the college believed that the same faculty members should teach all cohorts of students if at all possible. However, the excessive use of teaching reassigned time to coordinate administrative functions prevented this from happening on many occasions. As a result, open sections were assigned to adjunct faculty in a piecemeal fashion. The rise of the number of adjunct faculty at Guttman was in direct contradiction to the original intent of the college's model that recognized the benefit of having full-time faculty teach the same students across an entire year. Certainly, Guttman hired and retained a corps of capable adjunct faculty, several of whom were eventually hired as full-time instructional staff, but the college was slow to correct the problem that led to these necessary hires. By and large, the instructional efficacy of the FYE deteriorated after 2012 because Guttman could not maintain consistent staffing patterns across the Houses. Instead, adjunct faculty, who were not compensated to participate in weekly team meetings and who did not have consistent communication or relationships with other faculty in the House, struggled to effectively coordinate lessons. Instead, components of City Seminar lacked integration, and students struggled to recognize the sections as parts of a whole course. Adjunct faculty have, however, been incredible collaborators and instructors. Their contribution to the development of the college must be acknowledged and celebrated. The reason by which the number of adjunct faculty teaching in the FYE has grown speaks to a flaw in the college's operational model. The flattened administrative structure, lack of departments, and inconsistent responsibilities of senior leadership created a situation whereby the vacuum of responsibilities had to be filled by faculty.

As Guttman and colleges across the country now face debilitating budget cuts caused by the economic shutdown from the global COVID-19 pandemic, there is fiscal impetus to restructure the administrative functions of the faculty. In response to CUNY's central office mandate that colleges reduce operating budgets by 10% for the 2020–2021 academic year, Provost Wach has already determined that reassigned time for administrative responsibilities will be reduced by close to half. Certainly, this strategy will help to shrink overhead, but how the institution will handle the distribution of labor is still in question. There are several opportunities for reimagining faculty administrative leadership at the college. The number of students and the college's inability to expand enrollment in the foreseeable future necessitates a restructuring of faculty/administrative leadership roles. At present, each program of study has a program coordinator. Each program coordinator is assigned between six and nine credit hours of reassigned time. This reduces the coordinator's teaching load substantially and requires the college to fill the gaps with adjunct faculty. Additionally, the FYE has traditionally offered multiple leadership opportunities for faculty. Recently, the college appointed a program coordinator to oversee the scheduling and programming of all the courses in the first year while retaining a separate coordinator for Ethnographies of Work. Although these positions are excellent service opportunities for faculty, they are not fiscally sustainable nor are they operationally sound. As the college faces substantial budget reductions in the coming year, the academic leadership structure must be changed to reflect the current fiscal climate. To better streamline decision-making and reduce the costs associated with reassigned time, the college might consider appointing two faculty leaders, one to oversee the FYE and one to lead the programs of study. Each of these faculty could be provided with significant reassigned time to lead the administration of the college's two academic areas. These faculty leaders would then report directly to the dean of faculty and academic affairs, reducing the complexity and cost of the leadership structure.

Equity and Diversity

For three years, the college has been actively engaged in work related to equity and diversity. Dr. Lavita McMath Turner has spearheaded a number of programmatic initiatives aimed at addressing institutional racism at Guttman. Workshops with external consultants like Jonathan Poullard, Dr. Yolanda Sealey-Ruiz, and Dr. Tia Brown McNair have been aimed at identifying areas in the structure and culture of the college where implicit bias and institutional racism act as barriers to student success. Not only do these negative sociocultural assumptions impact student performance, but they also create chasms in how staff and faculty engage with and feel a part of the institution. During Dr. McMath Turner's tenure at Guttman, faculty and staff have participated in a wide range of workshops and seminars aimed at dismantling structural racism. For many, these opportunities have been uplifting and nurturing. For some, however, this type of engagement has further fueled animosity along racial lines. In January 2020, Drs. Sealey-Ruiz and Brown McNair addressed the Guttman community at an All-College Meeting. Dr. Brown McNair focused on the areas of the academic framework, including the college's concept paper, that need to be reconsidered in light of data that show inequities in student outcomes. Dr. Sealey-Ruiz, in turn, encouraged faculty and staff to dig deeply into their own beliefs and assumptions about students and the institution to help heal the fractured institutional culture. Feedback from participants at the daylong meeting illustrated the conflicting opinions about the gravity of institutional racism at the college. Some participants lauded the honesty conveyed by both of the speakers and the willingness of their colleagues to be vulnerable in an emotionally charged space. Others indicated that the speakers were repetitive and that they felt attacked by constant conversations about racism. Also, some respondents indicated that being challenged to consider the impacts of institutional racism was an assault on faculty teaching practices and implied that courses were laced with low expectations. The fractured responses made clear the depth of structural racism that ran through both the academic enterprise and Guttman's workplace culture.

White faculty and staff at Guttman must continue their own personal anti-racist journeys, but the institution can act from a policy standpoint to squarely address the inequities that persist as a result of structural racism. As a transfer preparatory college, Guttman should be committed to providing a strong general education foundation for its student body. As has been discussed previously in this book, the college and its faculty must pivot from a pedagogy of skills building to content mastery. Research about how to shrink racial achievement gaps suggests that students who have been marginalized by systemic racism in education must be exposed to challenging coursework that encourages them to continually meet more complex and rewarding challenges. Too often, students of color from low-income backgrounds are dragged down by institutions that assume they cannot do the work because of who they are. The cycle reproduces itself and drowns institutions in weak standards and unmotivated students. Unlike many community colleges across the country, Guttman's mission is not multifaceted. It is not designed to prepare students for specific vocations, nor does it have the capacity to serve part-time students who are hoping to brush up on professional skills through continuing education. Guttman is equipped to prepare traditional community college students for transfer. The equity work that has been underway at Guttman is, in large part, an effort to reorganize the institutional culture around this reality. However, the college must be able to shift away from the deficit framework that was delivered in the concept paper. In order to do so, it must examine data alongside individual and institutional beliefs about students.

The next stages of the equity work at Guttman are about significant policy change. The consultants have helped the college community understand that institutional racism is impacting the student experience. Tough policy decisions will help the college move from dialogue into action. Many of the policy changes that are necessary have been discussed in this book in detail. Guttman must address its structural policies and practices. When the college was founded, there were a number of structural dimensions framed in the concept paper that have been essential to its first decade in operation. In order to achieve its lofty goal of increasing completion rates, Guttman set itself apart from the rest of the university and circumvented traditional institutional practices that uniformly apply to the other community colleges. For example, until 2020, the college had not allowed students to transfer into the college from another CUNY or external institution nor had it permitted students to apply already earned college credits to courses at Guttman. The rationale has been that students who decide to enroll at Guttman should all have the same educational experience, meaning everyone must take the same classes at Guttman regardless of what credits they bring to the table. In New York City, many students have the opportunity to take college courses in high school and enter college with credits in English, math, and other general education subject areas. CUNY policy is that these credits be evaluated and offered equivalency by each of the colleges separately. What qualifies for an advanced math course at Bronx Community College may be very different at Hostos Community College. Guttman determined, however, that no transfer credits would be applied to courses in the first year. Evidence from student applications suggested that many more students than originally imagined were enrolling at Guttman with transfer credits in math, English, and other subject areas. Since Guttman had established an institutional policy prohibiting students from being awarded transfer credit for FYE courses, individuals were forced to retake critical gateway courses for which they already had credit. The issue of the college's resistance to applying transfer credit for incoming freshmen dovetails with the remedial nature of the FYE. Not only were students not receiving credit that would have been applied to their transcript at another CUNY community college, but these students, who had already successfully completed college-level general education courses, were also required to enroll in the extraneous developmental skills hours that were built into the first-year courses. Guttman, in turn, created barriers to student success that slowed progress toward a degree and prevented students who had already earned college credits from advancing in their coursework.

The work involving equity in the college's formative years converged during the COVID-19 pandemic that began in March 2020, a topic that will be discussed extensively in the next chapter. The real possibility of substantial budget cuts forced senior leadership to accelerate plans to modify the curriculum to be more cost-effective and supportive of student success. In a note to the faculty in June 2020, Dean of Faculty and Academic Affairs Nicola Blake wrote that incoming students who are proficient in developmental skills can no longer be required to enroll in the components of City Seminar that are billed to financial aid as remedial hours. Additionally, she accurately noted that students who are assessed as benefiting from some form of remediation under the new CUNY standards can acquire those skills in statistics and in English composition, both of which have developmental hours built into them for students with remedial needs. Therefore, as she concluded, City

Seminar requires a wholesale restructuring to promote equity in terms of instruction and to align the number of contact hours with the number of credits earned so that all students are earning college-level credit for the time they spend in the classroom. This will radically shift the culture of Guttman Community College away from one of deficit and inability. By recognizing students' educational achievements, through concrete policy change, the curriculum can be reconstructed to serve as a rigorous preparatory foundation for transfer. This will help Guttman grow toward a different and more equitable future.

Governance and Administration

Issues around college governance foregrounded this book and a great deal of time was spent discussing the challenges Guttman has faced in developing an appropriate governance plan for a small college within a large university structure. There are, however, additional points to be made with regard to how the college should consider revising the governance and administrative apparatus to better support the flow of decision-making and broad institutional change. Since the college has, for many years, been in start-up mode, it has been incredibly challenging for individuals to establish their unique roles in the institution. The lack of bureaucratic and academic structure has resulted in cross-pollination, which has often led to duplicative efforts in multiple arenas. This section will focus on how the decision-making structure should be reorganized to resolve such issues that have prevented necessary changes from being made as a result of incomplete or inaccurate information.

The leadership structure of the Office of Academic Affairs includes the vice president for academic affairs and provost and three deans. When Provost Joan Lucariello first hired the three deans, each was assigned areas of oversight. Laura Gambino was responsible for assessment and instructional technology, Patricia Price managed the programs of study and faculty personnel matters, and Marissa Schlessinger oversaw the FYE and program scheduling. However, and because of the integrative nature of the college, those areas of responsibility converged with other areas quite often, making it difficult for each dean to establish managerial authority over her portfolio. One example of where roles and responsibilities ineffectively converged was in the area of assessment. Since so much of the college's formative documents and planning focused on learning outcomes assessment as an essential component of the institutional mission, there was a great deal of energy around such work. When Gambino was appointed as dean, her role as assessment coordinator for the college interfaced directly with Elisa Hertz, director of the CCE. The concept paper indicated that the CCE was to be responsible for the assessment work at the college. However, there was a disjuncture between how the Office of Academic Affairs and the CCE should coordinate assessment efforts. The Office of Academic Affairs believed that student learning outcomes assessment work should be managed by academic leadership while Hertz and the CCE understood their role to be the appropriate facilitators. The struggle here was not one of personalities or professional territory but one of ill-defined spaces within the institution. The CCE was imagined as a hub of research and assessment that would interface with all areas of the college community. However, and as has been described elsewhere in this book, the CCE never grew to its full capacity. Hertz, however, had substantial experience in institutional and program assessment. In turn, Gambino was hired explicitly to lead the development of the learning outcomes assessment plan for the college. These roles were largely duplicative, and efforts were wasted attempting to sort out which area was responsible for assessment. As a result, outcomes assessment work at Guttman has been largely superficial in nature. The lack of coordinated effort among units and without a consistent leader in this area caused the college's attempts to organize an effectual assessment framework to falter.

The Office of Student Engagement (OSE) has been critical in promoting student success but has often found itself at the center of many debates about the roles and responsibilities of faculty and staff in student learning. One of the most complicated components of initiating the Gutttman model from an organizational standpoint was how OSE and the Office of Academic Affairs were to work with one another. Unlike many colleges where student affairs is a separate division of the university bureaucracy, Guttman's OSE was intended to be an integrative component of the academic enterprise. For many years, Dean of Student Engagement Charles Pryor reported to the provost. Eventually, Dean Pryor was made a member of senior staff, a leadership shift that moved OSE out from under the oversight of academic affairs. Yet the consistent interaction between advisors, faculty, and students remained an important element of the model that most of the community believed should be preserved. As was discussed in the chapters about the FYE, advisors, all of whom report to senior leadership in OSE, meet weekly with faculty on the instructional teams and facilitate a required, noncredit section of the first-year core curriculum. The challenges with this arrangement, however, have stemmed from how institutional culture has formed around this practice. As integrated members of the instructional staff, advisors often carry the dual role of faculty member and counselor. Students rely on their advisors to help them with academic planning but also how to handle the pressures of the classroom, including conflicts with other students and their instructors. Faculty members, in turn, lean on advisors to help them navigate complex student issues ranging from disengagement in the classroom to concerns about a student's personal life. For many advisors, this bifurcated role creates a great deal of stress and has led to burnout and high turnover.

Lessons for Higher Education

As new programs and institutions evolve, there should be an expectation that start-up initiatives mature into the foundations of college culture. During Guttman's planning phase, there was a strong insistence that the college be responsive to real-time data. However, the college did not organize a comprehensive assessment plan to evaluate the model, a blind spot that has been discussed previously in this book. What has been most striking, however, are the beliefs about the efficacy of the model that have filled the data void. Since there has been no evaluation of the college, attempts to make changes to the model have largely relied on anecdotal evidence or knee-jerk reactions to isolated data points, such as student success rates in a specific course. The absence of a structured and systematic feedback loop has permitted individual faculty and staff opinions to serve as data. Not only have some decisions, and in Guttman's case, indecision, rested on conjecture, these personal narratives have bifurcated the cultural fabric of the college between those who believe the college's model is flawed and those who wish to preserve it. Certainly, the history of higher education in the United States is full of opinion, individual interests, and resistance to change from various institutional bodies, but the Guttman story offers an example of what happens to institutional culture and a college's ability to change when the only evidence available is personal opinion.

The normal tensions that occur between faculty and administration have been exacerbated at Guttman. Without appropriate evaluation data early on in the college's evolution, a small cadre of faculty and senior leadership crafted an outward-facing message that the college was successfully executing its experimental model, and with incredible results. On many fronts, this façade was organized with a strong comparison to the "traditional" community college whose academic and bureaucratic flaws had failed generations of students. Behind this moniker of separateness was a steadfast belief that Guttman was the way of the future. However, and as many leaders at CUNY recognized, the Guttman model could only be heralded as a success if it could be applied to several thousand students. A boutique institution with under 1,000 in enrollment could not be characterized as a watershed shift in policy or practice. Many at Guttman, though, viewed the college's high graduation rates as a signal that the model was working and compared the 50% three-year completion numbers to those of its peer colleges who struggled to reach 20%. Critical to this comparison, though, and apart from the very small student body at Guttman, were several distinct requirements that were unavailable to larger, comprehensive community colleges. Guttman's full-time requirement meant that it attracted a student body whose primary function was to attend college. Other community colleges across the system enrolled a far more diverse cross-section of the college-going population, including scores of part-time students who came to college without the intention of earning a degree. Guttman was intended to serve a very narrow purpose in the broader mission of community college education. As a result, it was difficult and perhaps unwise to compare its metrics with those of other colleges.

Designing a radical new program or institution, especially in an era where quantitative metrics are widely used as evidence of success, leadership must be committed to providing consistent and transparent feedback regarding performance and effectiveness. There are a number of reasons why this is important ranging from ethics to fidelity of mission. Yet in a climate where the purse strings of a college are largely controlled by the political infrastructure of state and municipal governments, honest reporting of data is critical to maintaining financial solvency. During challenging economic times, colleges have been called into question with regard to their outcomes. If an institution lacks substantial evidence to justify its existence its livelihood could be jeopardized. The ASAP program, which has been discussed widely in this book as an example of a successfully evaluated and operationalized community college reform program, is facing a possible set of devastating fiscal cuts as a result of the COVID-19 pandemic. The proposed budget cuts come from New York's City Hall and threaten to slash $20 million in operating funds from the program this coming fall. ASAP, which has largely been successful because of significant investment from New York City dating back to the mayoralty of Michael Bloomberg, will not be able to enroll a freshman class in fall 2020 if the cuts are approved.[3] ASAP has widely reported on the efficacy of its program and has relied on external evaluators like MDRC and the CCRC to substantiate its claims through rigorous assessment of outcomes. Although ASAP faces an uncertain future, it has leverage to legitimize its program's future. Guttman, however, does not. Budget cuts stemming from the pandemic will force every institution to vie for baseline support. No doubt evidence of impact will be called into question by legislators and senior university officials whose job it will be to apportion a very small fraction of what was available to the colleges only a few short months ago. In the political jockeying that lies ahead, ASAP can provide a comprehensive historical account both of its evolution and its impact on student success. These evaluation reports are crucial to demonstrate why funding should be allocated to the program. When Guttman is forced to advocate for itself in the fiscal whirlwind that is sweeping the system, it will only be able to rely on anecdotal evidence to support why it should continue to receive the kind of funding to which it has become accustomed. Additionally, recent access to university-level data that shows Guttman students underperforming at their transfer institutions will raise red flags against a backdrop of requests for continued funding.

A college's ability to demonstrate evidence of sustained, positive impact on student learning is essential to its long-term institutional health. Periods of economic prosperity are typically followed by severe fiscal downturns, or so the case has been over the past half-century. Institutions and programs that have been proven to be effective in enhancing student performance are not immune to severe budget cuts but are far better positioned to make substantiated claims for why they should not be entirely eliminated. Guttman Community College missed the mark in this area by not investing in a rigorous evaluation of the model. Not only has this evidence vacuum divided the college politically, but it has also prevented the institution from making the necessary changes early on that could have bolstered its relevance and standing in the university community. Although there may be a desire by some to rely on a narrative of success rather than honestly attending to less attractive metrics, it is by responding to blind spots in programs that leadership is able to remedy problems and create better, more stable pathways for the future.

Notes

1. Memorandum, *Policy for the Use of CUNY's Proficiency Index in Developmental Education Assignments* (New York, NY: City University of New York Office of Academic Affairs, 4 September 2019), 2.
2. Memorandum, 3.
3. Madeline St. Armour, "Looming Budget Cuts Threaten Proven Program," *Inside Higher Ed*, June 30, 2020, www.insidehighered.com/news/2020/06/30/experts-worry-proposed-cuts-cuny-asap-foreshadow-trend-higher-ed.

6   The Way Forward

When I was first organizing the proposal for this book, my inclination was that the postsecondary system in the United States was settling into the changes it had made during and after the recession. I imagined, if only for a moment, that we were immersed in a stable period, even if the vitriol and political dogma swirling across the globe illustrated otherwise. On March 9, however, I opened the meeting of Guttman's Scalability Taskforce with an acknowledgment that the stock market was in freefall. For several weeks, a novel coronavirus had been picking up pace from its epicenter in Wuhan, China, and was rapidly spreading across Europe and headed toward the United States. That morning was the first day my college community realized it was in the crosshairs of a global pandemic. What transpired over the course of the next few weeks was cataclysmic as contemporary history was rewritten and the world shut down.

On March 11, Guttman Community College closed its doors. COVID-19, the name given to the disease caused by the novel coronavirus, had forced universities across the country and the globe to prematurely end in-person classes for the spring semester. Andrew Cuomo, governor of the State of New York, announced that all public universities in the state would shift to online learning for the remainder of the semester. On the day of the announcement, we all thought the governor's response was an extreme reaction to a problem we imagined would resolve itself in a few short weeks. In fact, Governor Cuomo's decision was muted in comparison to the other radical alterations to daily life we would encounter in the weeks and months ahead. As the first cases arrived at U.S. hospitals on the East and West Coasts, movie theaters, gyms, offices, and restaurants closed. Economic life in the United States was decimated in a matter of days. Unsurprisingly, New York City became the North American epicenter of the virus, and the number of predicted cases threatened to overwhelm the already fragile health-care system. In Manhattan, busy streets went quiet except for the continuous roar of ambulance sirens ferrying the sick to local emergency rooms. The naval hospital ship, *U.S.S. Comfort* arrived in New York Harbor, passing the Statue of Liberty on its way to the West Side piers, and the Jacob Javits Center was converted into a field hospital to treat coronavirus patients. We wore masks. Broadway went dark indefinitely. The world stopped.

There was a flurry of web activity at CUNY and Guttman, however. From our homes, we quickly responded to the governor's order to continue the semester in an online format. In just a few days' time, CUNY reconfigured thousands of in-person classes so that students could access lessons virtually. Guttman Community College responded swiftly. Faculty and advising staff quickly moved courses into digital formats using platforms that students already had experience using, including the ePortfolio system and Blackboard. After a few days of recalibration, classes resumed. Weekly instructional team meetings continued in Microsoft Teams and Zoom. Governance slowly reemerged from a short hiatus, and committee work made its way through the college council. But little was the same.

In New York City, early pandemic data showed that communities of color were disproportionately affected by the virus. Wealthy White New Yorkers fled to second homes, vacation towns, and extended families far from the density of the city. Many of those who remained were essential workers: paramedics, nurses, delivery staff, grocery store employees, and transit officials. Many of those who remained to tend stores and look after New Yorkers were from the lowest socioeconomic groups and overwhelmingly non-White. What shone through the darkness was the critical mass of people of color who carry the city day by day. A new era of White flight emerged in the midst of a global health crisis, spotlighting the horrific depths of income inequality in one of the world's richest cities. We at Guttman felt those effects enormously. Every day we heard stories of students whose family members passed away and others who feared for their parents and grandparents and brothers and sisters working on the front lines to fight the virus. Over the course of the spring semester, we struggled with attendance and communication and pared down our classes to the very basics. Not only were our students and their families positioned in the crosshairs of the virus but also resource disinvestment played a role in how students were able to complete their coursework.

Community college students across the country rely on campus-based resources to sustain their educational trajectories. Students with limited access to home computers and Wi-Fi come to campus libraries to complete their assignments. When the pandemic hit New York City, our students were confined to their apartments. Although some students adjusted to the abrupt change in course delivery, some did not. For those of us who believe that community colleges are spaces of radical transformation, the realities of life in quarantine emphasized the kinds of inequities we work day in and day out to fight against. Most of us believed that the spring term would be one of a kind, and the pandemic would run its course by the start of summer. At the time of writing, the calendar is rapidly approaching the start of June. New York City is still under strict stay-at-home orders. Although there are signs of life emerging, including a return of fabled Midtown traffic, many months remain of harsh restrictions on everyday life. As a result, CUNY is preparing for a fully online fall semester.

There are a number of implications to the decisions that loom for CUNY and the postsecondary system in the coming months. Already some major systems, including the University of California network, have determined that the large majority of courses will be remote in the fall. Students who imagined starting college in a residential setting are finding a growing chorus of schools informing families that coursework will be completed from home until such a time as the public health situation allows for a slow return to campus. Other colleges are taking a more liberal approach. Some are stating that there will be a traditional, on-campus semester, while others are proposing a hybrid approach to limit the number of students in classrooms. Governor Cuomo has provided daily information through extended press conferences, discussing the metrics associated with the coronavirus pandemic. In April, the White House issued guidance to the states on how they might consider reopening as new cases and hospitalizations subside. As the epicenter of the American pandemic, New York City was slow to meet its required thresholds for reopening. As states lifted lockdown orders, the five boroughs remained in isolation. For the CUNY administration, hopes of a traditional fall semester faded as summer rose above Manhattan.

At Guttman, there was little in the way of hope for students returning to campus in autumn. Even if the university permitted a hybrid-online semester, Guttman's space constraints presented challenges to the government's mandate of social distancing. I have not spent a great deal of time in this book discussing Guttman's issues around space. I have believed it imperative that the institution aggressively evaluate its present practices and make necessary adjustments to the model before it considers enrollment growth. However, the coronavirus pandemic has compounded an already difficult living situation. Guttman's office building on 50 West 40th Street in Midtown is already overcrowded. Faculty and staff share office space, often with over a dozen professionals occupying cubicles in a single room. Classrooms, which originally fit up to 40 students, have

The Way Forward 101

been carved in half to make room for additional smaller classes. There is little space for students to do work, socialize, or work with faculty and advisors. The cramped environment is a prime space for disease to spread. Yet the operationalization of the Guttman model is predicated on the high-touch student experience. Faculty/staff/student relationships are central to the principles of learning at Guttman. The FYE, documented at length in this book, requires a substantial amount of integrated labor hours with faculty and staff communicating regularly, meeting weekly, and interweaving assignments and class themes so that material is taught with a unified approach. Although this book largely recommends that those structures be revised to support a college of transfer-focused students, faculty continue to retain much of the original structure despite challenges to its efficacy. The pandemic has instigated further challenges to the educational framework.

Much of Guttman's coursework will be taught remotely in the 2020–2021 academic year. Unless there are radical shifts in the political and health-care orders or a viable vaccine is readied expediently, there is little opportunity for students and staff to safely repopulate the campus. This has forced faculty and administration to begin reconfiguring the Guttman model for a fully online environment. There are a number of issues emerging from this reality. First, the New York State and City budgets promise to be catastrophic. Guttman is predicted to have to cut over $2 million in costs over the 2020–2021 academic year. This includes the elimination of many part-time and vacant positions. Second, there is belief across the country that postsecondary enrollment in the fall 2020 term will be low as students defer admission until the following year or decide to not enroll at all. Third, Guttman and other colleges predict high attrition for continuing students. Those who were enrolled during the spring semester when the pandemic forced classes online received a substandard education and may not want to repeat that in the fall. Lastly, Guttman is unable to predict whether the university will mandate additional staffing cuts, including full-time faculty. The Professional Staff Congress of CUNY, the university's powerful faculty union, has launched a preemptive ad campaign denouncing campus leadership for considering adjunct nonreappointments and course cuts. In late May 2020, John Jay College of Criminal Justice, Brooklyn College, and the College of Staten Island had all stated publicly that part-time instructional staff layoffs were imminent. Although Guttman had not yet made any firm decisions regarding staffing for the 2020–2021 academic year, it had announced to the community that resources would be heavily depleted.

The devastating budget year will undoubtedly reshape the curriculum. My thinking throughout this book and in my work as a faculty member at

Guttman assumed that the college would continue on an upward evolutionary track toward eventual enrollment growth. Scaling up the college, now, seems farther out of reach than ever. The central office is in triage mode and will be for the foreseeable future. The pandemic has forced the university into a reactionary mindset rather than a visionary one. These periods of crisis management are not often punctuated with large-scale capital projects but there have been exceptions to this rule. Demand for community college education during the recession era prompted the creation of programs like ASAP and the formation of Guttman Community College. Demand for community college degrees rose exponentially during this period. Whether we see the same kind of demand during this economic downturn is uncertain. Unlike the Great Recession, this economic collapse was deliberately manufactured to avoid a full-scale public health disaster. At the time of writing, there is 20% unemployment in the United States as Main Street waits for the all clear to go back to work. Turning back on the lights will be much slower than the speed at which they were turned off. Guttman cannot assume that people who are out of work will rush the community college system as they did at the start of the 21st century. Instead, the college will be forced to adjust its curricular offerings to prepare for multiple potentialities.

In order to diversify its admissions pool, Guttman will need to relax the full-time requirement in the first year. There is substantial research, much of which is discussed in this book, that points to better outcomes for students who enroll in a community college full time. Guttman should not abandon its commitment to providing structures that support full-time students. There is, however, a population of students who would greatly benefit from Guttman's supportive model who cannot make the commitment to enroll in a full-time degree program that requires them to spend much of their days on campus throughout the calendar year. This is a time for Guttman to seize on opportunities to reorganize the curriculum to create multiple pathways through the college. Not only will this widen opportunities for recruitment, but it also will help the college adapt its curricula and student support services for students with varying needs. The college might also benefit from offering a partially online version of its academic programs for students who are interested in distance learning. Certainly, Guttman was designed to attract a specific student body, but after almost a decade in operation and as a result of the aftermath of the pandemic, the college must find ways to evolve beyond this narrow focus.

This will require a wholesale reconfiguration of the FYE. A good deal of time has been spent in this book critiquing the FYE. My beliefs are grounded in specific data points that illustrate how and why the FYE must change in order to be effective. The COVID-19 pandemic has forced us to work with less and has taught us that excess does not equal opportunity. The Guttman model was built on excess. Data indicate that the majority of Guttman students do not require additional hours of remediation. CUNY has made substantial gains in how proficiency is determined, but Guttman has been slow to adjust its curriculum to match these shifts in policy. The excess contact hours that were intended to support remediation are no longer necessary, yet they remain. Each of these hours is costly, for the student and the institution. They are unnecessary. The budget crisis that is currently on our doorstep will teach us that investment in unnecessary excess is unnecessary. There have been a number of reasons given to maintain the additional contact hours in the FYE, but it is no longer financially responsible to require additional hours for courses for which the basic reasoning is contradicted by years' worth of data.

Most importantly, Guttman students deserve to be rigorously and effectively educated. The pandemic has shown us, once again, that communities of color have been historically harmed by a lack of resources and cultural beliefs that reproduce generational violence. Guttman's first-year curriculum is causing harm to its students. The assumptions about race, social class, and ability that were introduced in the concept paper resulted in a curriculum that leaned on additional classroom hours to correct perceived deficiencies. Guttman students and institutional data have proven these assumptions to be false. Again and again, students ask for a curriculum that will better prepare them for their baccalaureate studies. It is the college's obligation to challenge the forms of structural racism that prevent students of color from accessing challenging curricula. The pandemic tells us that the time is now.

Provost Wach has made a bold effort to reshape the curriculum during the spring 2020 semester. During his time as provost, Wach has overseen the reduction of the number of contact hours in City Seminar from 10.5 to 6. Most recently, he eliminated the Studio component of City Seminar, effective in fall 2020. The reduction in contact hours has been in response to accurate student data. The process by which this has unfolded, some of which has happened virtually through the pandemic, has been complicated. Certain faculty and administration remain committed to the original model. There are various reasons for this, many of which have to do with beliefs in certain constructivist pedagogical traditions. There are also professional benefits that come along with teaching in the first year. Faculty are awarded one full course release for their participation in the instructional team over the course of the entire academic year. Additionally, instructional team leaders are compensated with additional reassigned time. Since the required teaching load for community college faculty is 24 credit hours annually, reductions in teaching are welcome. As a result, Provost Wach has seen substantial pushback from the faculty as a result of his decision to reduce the contact hours in City Seminar. For some, this effort is akin to a dismantling of the framework from which the college was built.

Protests

As the first summer of the new decade dawned, America's racial tensions boiled over on city streets that had, for months, been eerily quiet. The nation abruptly lurched from an Orwellian silence to an enraged, violent scream. A string of murders of Black men by White supremacists in Georgia and police officers in Minnesota ripped the veneer of unusual solitude to shreds. In what seemed like a flash, New York, Los Angeles, Las Vegas, Minneapolis, and other major urban centers across the country became scenes both of mass peaceful protest and violent action. Thousands of people marched over the Brooklyn Bridge into Manhattan, torching police cars, looting high-end retail stores along Broadway in SoHo, and burning trash where rush hour traffic once raged. For many, it seemed like an involuntary spasm, perhaps a reaction to being indoors for so long. But for those of us who are acutely aware of the historical oppression and systemic violence that has, for generations, been responsible for the murder of people of color, this was a reckoning long past due.

What emerged on a national and global stage as a reaction to centuries of violence and oppression was exactly what Guttman and other colleges around the country had been attempting to reconcile on their campuses. As a social institution, postsecondary education is often incorrectly touted as a mechanism of social mobility. Although there is potential for some to increase their lifelong earnings with a college degree, that ability is dictated by the individual's race. And college is not available in the same way to everyone. Cultural capital and exposure to high-quality material are often reserved for those who are able to enter the elite tiers of academia, which often comes with a hefty price tag. Community colleges across the country have been the centers of postsecondary stigma. Generations of data indicate that students who start at a two-year college are far less likely to earn a bachelor's degree than those students who started at a four-year college. The community college becomes a barrier to individual goals and ambitions.

In some ways, Guttman promised solutions to those problems. But it has found that its educational model continues to perpetuate systemic inequities in outcomes and, in other ways, has created new barriers that deter student success. We have found this to be the case primarily in our transfer outcomes. With such an expensive and labor-intensive model, students who leave Guttman should be outperforming their peers in GPA and credits accumulated. There has been a significant amount of dialogue on campus regarding the cultural narratives that uphold what many view as low expectations. What the national outcry puts into perspective is that segments of society are no longer willing to tolerate the oppressive treatment of people of color in this country. The visuals of protests cascading through the streets are representative of the smaller shifts in thinking and action happening in our institutions. Guttman's culture was organized around a misguided set of educational principles built on assumptions about race and ability. The conflict that has emerged on a campus signals a moment of reckoning. Just as the country can no longer tolerate the murder and oppression of people of color by the police and racist vigilantes, postsecondary education, our leaders, and our instructors can no longer participate in a project of racial discrimination. We must challenge our biases, our notions of exceptionalism, and our beliefs about deficit if we are, as a cultural institution, to eliminate the foundation of difference that has historically marginalized the students to whom we are responsible. The lessons learned at Guttman can be used across higher education as institutions take time to self-evaluate, identify inequities, and act.

Transition and Uncertainty

In December 2019, President Evenbeck announced his plans to retire at the conclusion of the academic year. This announcement marked the informal end to Guttman's adolescence. Evenbeck saw the college through the latter years of its planning phase, the growth of its faculty and student body, and through numerous periods of conflict and challenge, both internally and externally. In May 2020, the university announced that Dr. Doris Cintrón would be named interim president of Guttman Community College while the university conducts a full presidential search. Dr. Cintrón, previously senior associate provost at CUNY's City College, will formally begin her tenure at Guttman on August 1, 2020. Guttman's new interim president will face many of the challenges discussed in this book. She will do so with the backdrop of continued fears of the global pandemic and racial protests that swept America's cities at the start of the summer in 2020. The transition will be incredibly challenging for Interim President Cintrón as she navigates a return to campus and the apex of racial conflict in the city and at the college.

For Guttman to thrive, the new leadership must examine old beliefs and challenge the stereotypes that still persist and have thrived since the college's inception. I am convinced that Dr. Cintrón is the person to lead Guttman into its next phase of development. Her background as a capable and pragmatic administrator is precisely what the institution needs to steady its turbulent adolescence and address its problematic historical roots. Even though her leadership is poised to carry the college through this transitional period, there are many questions that still must be answered about Guttman's future. During the economic boom that swept the late teens, there was little indication from the CUNY central office that a permanent location for Guttman was a priority. In fact, questions relayed by Guttman faculty and administration regarding a facility were met with ambiguous responses by two CUNY chancellors. Over the course of its short history, it has been clear that Guttman is not a policy priority. Without additional physical space, Guttman cannot and will not grow. If that is the case, the cost of the institution relative to the number of students it can serve is difficult to justify. The current space at Bryant Park comes with a price tag of several million dollars per year. With fewer than 1,000 students enrolled, overhead costs are difficult to meet.

There are several opportunities for Guttman in the coming years. If it is not the plan of the central office to close the institution entirely, then there are creative possibilities to better align the Guttman mission to current university realities. With transfer as a central policy focus, and one that will no doubt remain of paramount importance in the coming years, Guttman could feasibly be absorbed by one of the four-year colleges and become its signature transfer institute. CUNY could dismantle the financially burdensome administrative structure of maintaining a fully operational college and retain the faculty, who would be charged with developing dual degree programs that align with the four-year college's majors. Students enrolling in the Guttman institute would not have the educational credentials to enroll directly into the four-year college but would be promised direct admission to a bachelor's degree program once they completed the required general education coursework and prerequisites in the institute. The university would have to work directly with the Stella and Charles Guttman Foundation to determine how CUNY might retain the endowment it was granted in 2013. The merger of Guttman with an already established four-year college would allow the principles of the college to support the mission of transfer and provide direct and accessible pathways for students through dual degree programs. Whatever the case, Guttman must be reimagined. Its inability to grow in size makes it vulnerable and resource-draining. In the coming years, it will be evident how the chancellor and his administration intend to rebrand the college.

Lessons for Higher Education

The story of Stella and Charles Guttman Community College illustrates a range of lessons for higher education. This book has focused on specific areas where Guttman's story of origin and early years of implementation illuminated blind spots in the thinking behind the concept of the college. Many lessons have been discussed at the conclusion of each chapter. As I write this final chapter and reflect on the issues that have been addressed in this book, I believe it appropriate and useful to integrate what has been said thus far into a final, summative recommendation. The central takeaway from this book is that the cultural, academic, and fiscal frameworks of Guttman Community College were *designed in reverse*. The planning team was charged with creating a college whose sole mission was to increase completion rates. From a theoretical and political perspective, this was a noble mission. However, unlike course syllabi, institutions cannot and should not be the product of backward mapping from such a narrowly defined outcome. There are a number of reasons why this is ill-advised. First, colleges are the reflection of the individuals whose thinking and expertise go into forming the cultural fabric and daily operations of these incredibly complex institutions. As such, eliminating the flexibility to create, assess, and revise academic content and institutional priorities, as has been the case at Guttman, prevents intellectual curiosity, vigorous debate over mission and principles, and fails to account for macro-social shifts in educational priorities. Although Guttman was engineered to be responsive to institutional data, its sole focus on graduating more students than its peer institutions meant that its curriculum became locked in place, unable to change. Second, the founding faculty were hired many years after planning for the college had begun. Although there was broad faculty input from the university community at large, the structures and pedagogical principles were determined by the administrators on the planning team. Since the planning team set its sights on developing a model that would increase completion rates, the curricular design of the college was organized in such a way that academic quality was considered secondary compared to efficiency. Whether or not the university intended to hire a cadre of senior faculty to be a part of the planning team is less important than how the curriculum was organized to support a utilitarian function—completion. Certainly, the founding faculty were charged with generating course material, but the framework for *how* the pedagogical apparatus of the college would be organized was a matter of function over substance. Third, the flattened administrative and governance structure was intended to curtail the substantial power departments and chairs had over the curriculum on other campuses.

One of the reasons given early on in the planning process for adopting a department-less college was to disperse power across the institution rather than having it consolidated in faculty chairs. From one perspective, this cultural shift was more egalitarian in approach and invited more voices into the decision-making process. From another, it attempted to subvert the authority of the faculty in curricular matters and instead hand such privileges over to the administration. In the case of Guttman, neither happened. The lack of structure proved, instead, to be chaotic for all parties. Often, faculty are blamed for preventing necessary reforms, especially if those reforms are generated at the top. In some cases, that may very well be true. At Guttman, though, necessary revisions to the model failed to be created or adopted because of bureaucratic inefficiency as a result of the flattened administrative and governance models. The college lacked expertise, usually found in department chairs, for how curriculum needed to move through the various phases of institutional- and university-level governance in order to be enacted. It also was short on long-range planning and vision because senior administrators, including Guttman's many provosts, became locked into addressing daily operational issues. Each time either the faculty or the administration attempted to make major changes to the academic enterprise, they fell short of reaching their intended goal. However, it was not because of strong, entrenched chairs or power-hungry administrators, it was simply because the college lacked the basic infrastructure to actualize such revisions.

There are considerable lessons to be drawn here. Certainly, any new institution should have a concise strategic plan and a realistic set of goals. But institution building requires forming a college from the inside out rather than in reverse. Retrospectively, Guttman would have organized a faculty planning team to complement university administrators who had been charged with executing Chancellor Goldstein's vision. Between 2007 and 2012, the faculty and administrators should have engaged in active conversations about remediation, transfer preparation, and degree mapping. At the same time, discussions about how to frame the institutional culture should have relied on the experiences of those already in the classroom at CUNY. Although there have been very public displays of faculty/administration rancor over CUNY's 60-year history, many faculty members deeply believe in the university's mission and are experts in how to effectively prepare students for further education and the workforce. This was largely ignored in the planning process, and it was overwhelmingly detrimental to the college's early operational phase. The nuances of how to educate an academically diverse set of students in a single classroom were missed. Instead, a generalized set of assumptions about race, ability, and socioeconomics foregrounded the college's opening. This steered faculty who came later toward negative stereotypes that have lowered academic standards and prompted poor outcomes both at Guttman and for the college's many transfer students.

In so many instances, reform initiatives are viewed as time sensitive. Presidents and academic leaders sometimes feel that if wholesale change is not enacted, they will lose already precarious budget lines and jeopardize their own professional standing. The lessons of Guttman should and must tell us that reform does not have to happen slowly but will be ineffective if the right people are left out of the discussion. Quite unfortunately, the reverse engineering of Guttman Community College was a result of the tightly organized group of individuals who were responsible for its creation. Divergent opinions were silenced, and incredible blind spots were missed in the years leading up to the opening of the college.

Afterword

When crafting the idea for this book, I did not imagine writing the preceding chapter as I have here. I could not have predicted what historic change would come to the world in just a few short months after I began writing. Yet as I sat down at my computer during the three-month lockdown prompted by the rapid spread of COVID-19, the tragedy and magnitude of death coupled with the fires of racial tension that spilled onto American streets seemed to truly encapsulate the Guttman story. For years, we fought in our own small sphere for racial justice and equity of outcomes for our students. It truly was a fight.

As I was closing out this book, I thumbed through old surveys from meetings and events Guttman had held in the years before COVID closed its doors. I was reminded in reading the comments about presentations of racial equity that the reckoning the country was facing had, at the microscopic level, been playing out in our classrooms, and meeting spaces, and library for years. I was reintroduced to the voices that anonymously shared how tired they were of hearing about racism and how offended they were that they were implicated in the college's faults. These words, harsh as they were, were also so familiar. The phrases were similar to those coming from our nation's leaders, from the podium at the White House, and from the cries of White supremacy under attack across the country. To ignore or silence the realities of racism, especially in an institution whose core tenet is to serve the public, is to act unjustly.

I'm certain that there are many who would argue that Guttman's model was transformative, that it graduated many more students than other CUNY community colleges, and that its focus on relationships helped students persist. This does not, however, tell the complete story. For many students, Guttman, and especially the FYE, perpetuated the stereotype of the unable and unwilling student. From its early planning stage, it crafted an image of a student who could not survive or thrive without what the institution had to offer. In order to justify low expectations, Guttman vilified academic disciplines. Content mastery and command of subject matter were removed from the curriculum in favor of a watered-down, skills-driven approach to community college learning. Instead of breaking down barriers, it created more.

Guttman's structural deficits were so acute that change was necessary in order for the college to remain at all viable. What was meant to be an experiment in innovative pedagogy and support services emerged as one of racial equality. Under enormous pressure from the college's administration and key faculty, Guttman had to change in order to better serve its students. In December 2020, a proposal reached the Curriculum Committee that offered the most comprehensive restructuring of the FYE in the college's history. Two new courses were designed, both titled American Studies rather than City Seminar, that focused on social justice, activism, and racial equality. The four-hour course will earn students three credits and makes no mention of remediation or developmental skills. When the proposal is passed by the college council, it will begin to shift the narrative of deficit to one of empowerment. This shift is not only responsible; it is transformative.

This new way forward was one of compromise. Under Dean Nicola Blake's leadership, the faculty responsible for the new set of courses were held to account for ensuring that the course was equitable for students and that it promoted the kinds of learning necessary for a collegiate environment. In collaboration with Lavita McMath Turner, Dean Blake was able to instill the principles of racial justice into the American Studies courses. The coming academic year will be a turning point for Guttman's entering students. They will be recognized as college students, capable of growth, and will have a curriculum that tells them that they have a right to learn.

I taught in New York City for ten years. My time at CUNY was a period of incredible change, both at CUNY and in the city. I cried as the waters from Hurricane Sandy flooded Lower Manhattan, stood silent on the tenth anniversary of the September 11 attacks, and celebrated at Stonewall when same-sex marriage was legalized. Each and every day, though, no matter the occasion, I went to Guttman. For each of us, the college was a personal project, one that we were deeply committed to and one that our lives were organized around. This book offers a harsh critique of the institution. This analysis is to plainly illustrate how structural inequities in higher education form and how they survive. It is also a portrait of how they can change.

There is a great deal to be learned from Guttman's short history. Perhaps the most striking takeaway is that Guttman ultimately recognized that the things it prided itself on the most were, in fact, the most harmful to its students. The core of the curriculum as imagined in the concept paper was corrosive. The belief that students were deficient permeated course content and assignment design. It set the tone for the institutional culture. In turn, what emerged ten years later as a revised first-year curriculum, flew in the face of those initial assumptions. The new American Studies courses that were proposed in 2020 are designed to give students voice and agency and to introduce them to complex histories, art, and literature so that they can be the leaders of change in the coming generation.

Through all of its trials, it was a privilege to be a part of this experiment. I am honored to have contributed to the shifting narrative, one where students are respected for who they are, what they know, and for what is possible. At this moment of great change, it is important to reflect on why we educate. For so many of us, we believe in the hope of the future and the power each of us has to shape our history.

Index

Accelerated Study in Associate Programs (ASAP) 3, 21, 26, 65, 96–97; assessment of 81; block scheduling framework 33; at Bronx Community College 38; creation of 102; high-quality community colleges through 9–10
Accuplacer software 85
adjunct faculty 48, 88–89
administration: and faculty conflicts at CUNY 42–44; and governance 93–95; at Guttman 53–59; work for faculty in 88–90
Admissions & Access peer mentors 40
advisors, faculty as 37–38
AFT/PSC resolution 42–43
Ambrose, Daniel 40, 56
American Association of Colleges and Universities (AAC&U) 7
ASAP see Accelerated Study in Associate Programs (ASAP)
Assessment and Professional Development Committee 61, 64
assessment days 74–76
associate's degree 5, 8, 15, 74

baccalaureate programs 9, 19, 77, 79
Bailey, Thomas 15, 24, 35–37
basic skills 30, 50, 65, 71, 87
Bass, Randy 15
Benjamin, Stephanie 48
Bill & Melinda Gates Foundation 6, 29
Blackboard 99
black students 5–6, 8
Blake, Nicola 57, 59, 65–66, 92–93, 111

block scheduling framework 9, 33, 34–35
Bloomberg, Michael 96
Broad Integrative Knowledge GLO 37
Bronx College and Lehman College 58
Bronx Community College 38, 92
Bronx Transfer Affinity Group (BTAG) 58, 79
Brooklyn College 101
BTAG see Bronx Transfer Affinity Group (BTAG)
budget reductions 82; COVID-19 pandemic 67, 89–90, 92, 96; on unnecessary investment 103
Buttet, Sebastien 61

cafeteria model 35
career-centric curriculum 19, 31, 43
Carnegie Corporation 29
Carnegie credits 25
CAT-W see CUNY Assessment Test in Writing (CAT-W)
CCE see Center for College Effectiveness (CCE)
CCRC see Community College Research Center (CCRC)
CEAFE see CUNY Elementary Algebra Final Exam (CEAFE)
Center for College Effectiveness (CCE) 40–42, 67, 94
Center for Inquiry & Innovation 41
Cintrón, Doris 105
City Seminar course 17, 31, 84; 12–6 calendar approach 43; depth-over-breadth approach 31;

English class in 30; evaluation of 65; Group Workspace 18, 19, 30, 43, 45; removal of reading/writing component 65, 72; revision of 58–59
City University of New York (CUNY): adjusting operational standards 49–51; baccalaureate programs 9, 19, 77, 79; and Bronx College and Lehman College 58, 79; co-requisite courses 58, 85–86; CUNY Start program 10, 85; developmental education at 9–10, 17, 72–73, 85, 87–88; enrollment 2–3, 16, 32–34, 48, 74; first-year core curriculum 17–18; precollege programs 14; Professional Staff Congress 101; remedial education 3, 8–9, 27, 71, 84–88; *see also* Accelerated Study in Associate Programs (ASAP); Guttman Community College
Cochran, Stuart 63
cohesive learning outcomes 36
Coleman, Mary 82
collaborative inquiry 42
College of Staten Island 101
college readiness, CUNY Start program 10
communication 31
Community College Research Center (CCRC) 7, 15, 96
community colleges 95–96; associate's degree 5, 8; budget reductions 67, 82, 89–90, 92, 96, 103; cafeteria model 35; completion rates 6, 9, 26, 87, 107; enrollment during Great Recession 2–3; flaws in 24; full-time enrollment 33; trouble spots in 15; using ASAP initiative, high-quality 3, 9; *see also* Guttman Community College
community days 76
COMPASS exam 46
completion rates, of community colleges 5–6, 9, 26, 87, 107
consortial faculty 48, 60
corequisite courses 58, 85–86
COVID-19 pandemic: budget reductions 67, 89–90, 92, 96; effects 98–100; enrollment during 67; reconfiguration of FYE 101–102

credit-bearing coursework, and developmental skills 24–25, 30, 84
critical assessment, of *NCC Concept Paper* 20–23
critical feedback, addressing 31
Crook, David 22, 25, 85
Cruz, José Luis 84
CUNY Assessment Test in Writing (CAT-W) 85
CUNY Elementary Algebra Final Exam (CEAFE) 45–46
CUNY Language Immersion Program 14
CUNY Prep Transitional High School 14
CUNY *see* City University of New York (CUNY)
CUNY Start program 10, 85
Cuomo, Andrew 98, 99
curriculum, in Guttman Community College: arts courses 76–77; assessment days 74–76; community days 76; Ethnographies of Work (Professional Studies) 18, 30, 31–32; first-year 44–47; FYE 69–74; Math Topics 18, 30, 32; misaligned 72; programs of study 74; rigorous assessment of 81–83; statistics courses 32, 42, 64; transfer 77–81; *see also* City Seminar course
Curriculum and Student Academic Support Committee 61

degree program *see* baccalaureate programs
developmental education 9–10; integrative model 17; *see also* remediation
developmental skills 16–18, 50, 87, 92; and credit-bearing coursework 24–25, 30, 84; integrated 1, 30, 41
Digication 39
digital courses 99
diversity 90–93

enrollment: COVID-19 pandemic 67; at CUNY 2, 16, 32–34, 48, 74; full-time 16, 32–34, 41, 55; during Great Recession 2–3; at Guttman 32–34, 66–67, 72, 95, 102; of nontraditional students 33–34
ePortfolios 8, 20, 37, 39, 47, 99

Index 115

equity, and diversity 90–93
Equity, Diversity, and Inclusion Taskforce 63
Ethnographies of Work 18, 30–32, 38; LABSS section of 40; learning workplace competencies 31
Evenbeck, Scott E. 42, 53–56, 105

faculty: adjunct 48, 88–89; and administration 42–44, 88–90; alternate roles and responsibilities 41; consortial 48, 60; contribution at Guttman 42; Office of Partnerships 31–32; and professional development 48, 58, 60, 63–64, 76; as student advisors 37–38; teaching in FYE 47–48; tenured 49; workload 25, 45
financial aids 25, 39
first-generation students 26
First-Year Experience (FYE) 19, 22, 29–32, 87–88; and CCE 40–42; curriculum 44–47; developmental education 87–88; Ethnographies of Work (Professional Studies) 31–32; full-time enrollment 32–34; guided pathways 35–37; institutional racism 26, 73, 77, 90–91; instructional team meetings 38, 47–48, 70; integrated advisement 37–38; leadership and staffing 47–48; learning communities and block scheduling 34–35; Math Topics course 32; peer mentoring 40; programs of study 74; reconfiguration of 101–102; revision of 69–74; student success advocate (SSA) 34, 38; see also City Seminar course
four-year colleges 8–9; transfer from Guttmann to 40, 78
free textbooks 9
full-time enrollment 16, 32–34, 41, 55
FYE see First-Year Experience (FYE)

Gambino, Laura 47, 57, 64, 67, 75, 93–94
Garvey, John 14
Gates Foundation 6
Gay, Geneva 26
GED programs 14
Global Guttman 59, 88

GLOs see Guttman Learning Outcomes (GLOs)
Goldstein, Matthew 1, 3, 8–9, 14, 16, 24, 53
Gonzalez-Stokas, Ariana 47
governance 21; absence of cohesive structure 43, 53; accreditation 63–66; and administration 93–95; personnel matters of faculty 59–61, 93; phased-in 66–67; plan in NCC 43–44; shared 61–63; task force 61–62
graduation rates, at Guttman 4, 11, 55, 78, 82, 96
Great Recession 2, 74
Group Workspace (City Seminar) 18, 19, 30, 43, 45
Grubb, W. Norton 15
guided pathways 16, 35–37
Guttman Community College 11–12; academic deficiencies 83; accreditation 63–66; Admissions & Access peer mentors 40; AFT/PSC resolution 42–43; assessment days 74–76; community days 76; enrollment 32–34, 66–67, 72, 95, 102; equity and diversity 90–93; experimental initiatives 67; faculty administrative work 88–90; full-time enrollment 32–34; governance and administration 43, 53, 66–67, 93–95; graduation rates 4, 11, 55, 78, 82, 96; guided pathways 35–37; implicit bias training 63–64, 73; inequities in student performance 58; institutional racism 26, 73, 77, 90–91; learning community and block scheduling in 35; Office of Student Engagement (OSE) 94; racial relations 58; remedial education 3, 8–9, 27, 71, 84–88; resisting transfer credits 92; shared governance 59, 61–63; student services 38; task force governance 62, 66, 98; technology at 39, 75; see also First-Year Experience (FYE)
Guttman Learning Outcomes (GLOs) 37, 75

Hertz, Elisa 67, 93–94
higher education 107–109; adjusting expectations 49–51; organizational

development 48–49; phased-in governance 66–67; planning perspectives 23–25; racist issues 26–27; rigorous assessment 81–83; in United States 95
high-impact practices (HIPS) 8, 60, 67
high-tech learning 20
Hill, Dalvin 74
HIPS *see* high-impact practices (HIPS)
Hispanic students 5–6, 8, 80
Hostos Community College 92

implicit bias training 63–64, 73
innovative pedagogy 7, 111
institutional racism 26, 73, 77, 90–91
instructional team meetings 38, 47–48, 70
Intellectual Skills GLO 37
intrusive advising 3, 27, 67
Ithaka S + R 67

John Jay College of Criminal Justice 101
Josiah Macy Jr. Foundation 29

King, Claire 47
Kingsborough Community College 34
Kyle, Peter 76

labor-intensive model 39, 56, 63
leadership and staffing 47–48
learning: communities 34–35, 45, 67; outcomes 7, 37, 47
Logue, Alexandra W. 46
low-income students 26, 91
Lucariello, Joan 56–57, 93

Makris, Molly 74
mandatory full-time enrollment 16, 41, 55
Math Topics course 18, 30, 32
McNair, Tia Brown 90
MDRC 67, 81, 96
Meade, Tracy 11, 14–15, 17, 20–21, 27
Mellow, Gail 22
Metropolitan Museum of Art 77
Microsoft Teams 99
Middle States Commission on Higher Education 63–64
Mogulescu, John 3–4, 9–11, 14, 20–21, 27
Morín, José Luis 42, 44, 56
Mucciolo, Larry 48, 60

NCC Concept Paper: critical assessment of 20–23; planning of 15–20
New Community College (NCC) *see* Guttman Community College
New York State Board of Regents 63
No Credit (NC) grade 50, 71
non-traditional students 26, 33–34

Obama, Barack 6
Office of Academic Affairs 38; leadership of 93–94; reconstruction of 57–58
Office of Partnerships 19, 31
Office of Student Engagement (OSE) 94
organizational development 48–49
OSE *see* Office of Student Engagement (OSE)

Patel, Bindi 56
Pathways Initiative 46–47, 80
peer mentoring 40, 47
Per Scholas 74
Peruggi, Regina 22
planning, of *NCC Concept Paper* 15–20; absence of critical race theory 26–27; blind spots in 50; critical assessment 20–23; history 14–20; perspectives for 23–25
portfolio-based assessment 25
Poullard, Jonathan 63, 90
Price, Patricia 57, 93
private donor funding 7
proactive advising 9
professional development 41, 48, 50, 58, 60, 63–64, 76
Professional Staff Congress 46
Professional Studies course *see* Ethnographies of Work
programs of study, at Guttman 74
protests, and racial tension 26–27, 104–105
Pryor, Charles 56, 94
public funding 7

quantitative reasoning 30–31, 64

Rabinowitz, Vita 84–85
racial discrimination 26–27, 104–105
Regents scores 85
remediation 3, 8–9, 27, 71, 84–88

Index 117

remote courses 99, 101
Roderick, Melissa 15, 22
Rojas, Estela 48
RPT document 60–61

Sanabria, Kim 48
SAT scores 85
Schaffer, Frederick 59–60
Schlesinger, Marissa 57, 93
Sealey-Ruiz, Yolanda 90
self-presentation 31
service learning 8, 47, 76
shared governance 44, 59, 61–63
skilled workforce, developing 6
skills-driven curriculum 27–28, 111
Slevin, James 17
SmartBoard technology 39
SSA *see* student success advocate (SSA)
staffing, for first-year 47–48
Starfish tool 39
statistics courses, in Guttman 32, 42, 64
Stella and Charles Guttman Foundation 106
Stroud, John 39
structural racism 4, 90–91, 103
students: advising services for 38; collaborative inquiry 42; of color 26, 80; completion rate of 7; failure rates of 39; laptops for 39; performance inequities at Guttman 58; workplace skills 18, 31
student success advocate (SSA) 34, 38, 45
Summer Bridge program 25, 29–30, 34, 47
Suss, Stuart 57, 59

teaching, and learning 41, 55, 60, 72
technology 7, 20, 39, 75

tenured faculty 49
transfer: credits 92; shock 40, 78
transfer-prep education 3, 15, 27
transfer students 38, 58, 77–81, 80; Bronx Transfer Affinity Group (BTAG) 58; to four-year college 8, 18, 27, 40, 77, 87; Pathways Initiative 46–47, 80; poor outcomes 69, 82; post-transfer GPA 79
transportation funds 9
Turner, Lavita McMath 57, 58–59, 73, 90, 111
two-year colleges 5; enrollment of nontraditional students 33–34; goals and practices of 6–7; *see also* community colleges
Tyner-Mullings, Alia 61

uncertainty 105–106
United States: higher education in 95; during recession 7, 98; unemployment in 102
University Faculty Senate 21, 22, 62

vocational education 2, 7, 27, 74

Wach, Howard 57–59, 72–73, 89, 103
Walker, Rebecca 63
white students 5–6, 80, 99
workplace skills, learning 18, 31
Wrigley, Julia 59

zero-credit courses 5, 8, 24–25; and co-requisite courses 58, 85–86; elimination of 16–17, 78
Ziehmke, Niesha 57
Zoom 99

Taylor & Francis eBooks

www.taylorfrancis.com

A single destination for eBooks from Taylor & Francis with increased functionality and an improved user experience to meet the needs of our customers.

90,000+ eBooks of award-winning academic content in Humanities, Social Science, Science, Technology, Engineering, and Medical written by a global network of editors and authors.

TAYLOR & FRANCIS EBOOKS OFFERS:

- A streamlined experience for our library customers
- A single point of discovery for all of our eBook content
- Improved search and discovery of content at both book and chapter level

REQUEST A FREE TRIAL
support@taylorfrancis.com